MW01107422

# Truth is Funnier Than Fiction

Humorous Essays and Stories
That Prove The Funniest
Things Happen in Real Life

By

Nancie Hudson

authorHOUSE™

1663 LIBERTY DRIVE, SUITE 200
BLOOMINGTON, INDIANA 47403
(800) 839-8640
WWW.AUTHORHOUSE.COM

First published by AuthorHouse 08/27/04

ISBN: 1-4184-9366-X (sc)

Printed in the United States of America
Bloomington, Indiana

This book is printed on acid-free paper.

Cover Design by Susan Holman

# Table of Contents

# Preface

The stories you are about to read are true. Most of the names have been changed or omitted to protect everyone except me from embarrassment.

But seriously, I've interviewed hundreds of people during my journalism career, and many of them have told me hilarious stories that I couldn't write about, because I'm a writer of serious business articles. So all these true, funny stories have been bouncing around in my brain for years, and the only way I can publish them is by changing the names.

"Truth is stranger than fiction," people say. I think the things that happen to people in real life are *funnier* than fiction because they are realistic and could happen to anyone. Like, the humorous things that happen when you're buying a car or starting a new job. I have also included some of my funniest adventures, such as my frugal European vacation, my move to a big city boomtown, and my foray into the radio business. Please be forewarned: some of these true stories can cause severe laughter. Because truth *is* funnier than fiction.

— Nancie Hudson, April 2004

# Chapter 1

## Making a Good Impression

A friend of mine, Cheryl, used to go shopping with her mom every week at a neighborhood grocery store where everyone knew everyone else. The front of this store had a wall of windows from floor to ceiling that people had to walk past in order to enter the store's front doors, and everyone inside the store routinely watched the parking lot activity through these windows while standing in the check-out lanes. One day when Cheryl and her mom, Edna, were walking past this wall of windows, Edna's pants suddenly dropped to her knees. Edna had been on a serious diet and had lost quite a bit of weight, so her pants were way too big for her. And she wasn't wearing any panties! She was wearing flesh-toned pantyhose, so she looked naked from the waist down.

Startled but still in need of groceries, Edna quickly pulled up her pants, and they went into the store and did their weekly grocery shopping, hoping no one had noticed the embarrassing incident. To prevent it from happening again, Edna bought a box of safety pins. When they got to the check-out lane and the cute bag boy Cheryl had a crush on was bagging their groceries, he carefully placed the box of safety pins in the bag and whispered to a humiliated Cheryl: "Your mom *needs* these."

Teenagers are acutely sensitive about being embarrassed, and not just by their parents, but by things they do when they're trying to impress their peers. A man who owns several restaurants told me that when he was in high school, he embarrassed himself, his coach and the entire hockey team at the start of a game because he was trying to show off. One by one, the other starting players had skated out onto the ice and formed a line in front of the crowd. Jerry was the starting center, so he was last. The announcer called out his name, "Jerry Webster, senior," and as the crowd applauded, Jerry skated out to the lineup as fast as he could and tried to do a fancy stop that he had practiced privately. This time it didn't work, and Jerry skated right into the player at the end of line. Like a row of dominos, the players fell over one by one until the entire starting lineup was sprawled out on the ice!

Police officers are always supposed to behave in a professional manner, but hey, they're only human. Like the police officer who was working the morning shift during a snowstorm that was so severe it prompted authorities to close the Interstate highway. He and several other cops had been drinking coffee in the local donut shop, and he had consumed *five* cups of coffee. So when he felt the urge to relieve himself while driving down the closed highway, it was *urgent*. Thinking he was completely alone, he pulled his car over to the shoulder, got out of the car and began taking care of business. "Now I used to play Fireman Bill," he recalled. "I wrote my name in the snow and experimented with how high and far I could spray my hose." Just as he was finishing his business, he heard someone say, "Officer! Officer!" Looking across the highway, he saw a man and a woman standing by a car that was stuck in the ditch, and the woman was laughing. "Could you please help us?" the man said. "When you're *done*, that is." He was so embarrassed that he *never* played Fireman Bill again.

We all *want* to make a good impression all the time, but things happen. Like the time I was starting a new job in a non-profit organization. I was told that I would be working closely with the board of directors, so I was eager to meet each person and make a good impression. One day right after I had finished eating leftover broccoli and rice casserole in the employee lunchroom, one of the board members and his wife came into the office. Enthusiastically I greeted them, introduced myself, shook their hands and froze my face in a big smile to let them know that I was a friendly person. They chatted with me and were very polite, but they kept staring at my mouth and then quickly looking away. After they left, the organization's president returned from lunch, and I told him that I had just met the board member and his wife. "You've got a green tooth," he said. "Did you just eat lunch?" I rushed into the ladies room, looked in the mirror and saw that a piece of broccoli had wedged itself in between two of my upper front teeth, completely covering a tooth. Yes, the new employee with the green tooth made a *great* first impression!

Starting a new job *is* exciting, sometimes too much so. Like the young college graduate who was starting her first full-time teaching job in an elementary school. She wanted to arrive early on her first day, so she packed her lunch in a hurry, throwing together a sandwich and grabbing some crackers and what she thought was a can of cold soda in the back of her refrigerator. At lunchtime, she went into the teacher's lounge and sat down at the big conference table where all the other teachers were eating. As she was unpacking her lunch, another teacher asked her how her first day was going so far. Ignoring her lunch momentarily, she chatted with the teacher about how well her morning had progressed. Then as she picked up her sandwich to take a bite out of it, she noticed that the can sitting on the table in front of her wasn't a can of soda — it was a can of beer!

The day I started my first full-time job as a clerical worker at a large insurance company, I was eager to impress everyone, including my supervisor, Maggie, and our office manager, Rich. I wanted to show them that I could figure things out on my own without asking a lot of stupid questions, but I couldn't figure out what to do with one piece of correspondence that had come in the mail. So I went into Rich's office and asked him what I should do with it. "File it in the circular file," he said. I walked all around the office and the conference room and looked everywhere, but the only circular file I saw was a big three-by-five-inch card rolodex, and you couldn't put an 8 1/2-by-11-inch letter in that. Finally, I gave up and asked Maggie where the circular file was because I couldn't find it. She laughed out loud, rocked back in her chair, and then told me to ask Rich. When I did, he laughed and said, "Nancie, the circular file is slang for the wastebasket, because the wastebasket is round. I was telling you that it's junk mail — just throw it away." From that day on, they teased me about the circular file.

When you start a new job, you always want to fit in and get along well with your new co-workers. That was certainly the case for Ned, a teenager whose parents own a small neighborhood grocery store. When he first started working in the store, the other teenage boys who were already working there as stockers and baggers played a joke on him. When he went into the men's employee bathroom in the back of the store, they pushed a heavy box in front of the door so he couldn't get out. He banged on the door loudly, someone let him out, and they all laughed about it. So the next day when Ned saw that the men's bathroom door was closed and someone was in there, he thought it was one of his buddies and decided to get revenge. He pushed the heavy box in front of the door and walked away laughing to himself. Then he saw that his friends were all stocking shelves in the store. Oops. *Who* was in the bathroom? Turns out, it was the older man who worked in the store's butcher shop as a meatcutter. Thinking that someone had deliberately played the prank on *him*, the man banged loudly on the door and yelled at the top of his voice, "Open this door *now*! I'm going to come out there and kick someone's butt!"

"You never get a second chance to make a good first impression," I've heard people say, and that's especially true during job interviews. A young woman who was being interviewed for an accounting job in the Texas savings and loan where I used to work had just walked into the vice president of accounting's office and sat down in the chair across from his desk when suddenly one of the buttons on her blouse popped off and fell on the floor, leaving part of her blouse open. Still poised and confident, she never flinched or missed a beat during the hour-long interview. And as she was leaving, she casually picked up the button and slipped it into her pocket. "That impressed me so much that I gave her the job!" the vice president told us. "I figured that if she could handle *that* with grace and dignity, she can handle anything."

But one of the most extreme examples of grace under pressure that I've ever heard was when Tom the Boy Scouts leader led his troop on an underground cave adventure in Indiana. "We don't *need* a cave guide," Tom told his troop and their parents. "I've been in this cave twice before, and I know all about caves, so *I'll* be our cave guide." Tom had been a Boy Scouts leader for seven years, so they believed him. On a Friday morning, Tom, the 12 boys, and three parents drove a caravan of cars from Michigan to southern Indiana for the day trip. But what was supposed to be a four- to five-hour hike through the underground cave turned into an eight-hour trek, because caves change. Sure, Tom had been in this same cave years ago, but it looked different now, and an abundance of rain had caused the water level of the underground river in the cave to rise. "I was the big fearless leader who knew all about caves, and then I couldn't find my way out!" Tom recalled.

The boys ranged in age from 11 to 15 and included Tom's 13-year-old son. Even though Tom was afraid, he didn't say a word to them about being lost because he didn't want them to panic. But *he* was on the verge of panicking, because they weren't prepared to spend the night in the cave. All they had brought was a few snacks and a little water, no sleeping bags, and the cave was wet, damp and chilly, around 54 degrees. Knowing that a search party wouldn't be sent into the cave by authorities until they had been missing for 12 hours, Tom knew he had to find a way out. So he went off by himself, a no-no in cave safety. He crawled through small openings on his hands and knees. He swam through the cold underground river, which was up to his neck. But by following the swollen river, he found a way out. Then he found his way back to where the boys were waiting and led them out of the cave. The parents who were waiting in their cars outside the cave were overjoyed when the group finally came out, and the boys never knew that they had been in danger. But Tom, who works as a professional photographer, said the whole time he was trying to find a way out, he kept thinking about the fact that the next morning, he had to be back in Michigan to photograph a wedding. "I was wondering how I was going to explain to this bride that I got stuck in a cave in Indiana!" he said.

# Chapter 2

# To Err is Human

True story in a family-owned party store: Two clerks called in sick on a Saturday morning when the family knew they were going to have an extremely busy day, so the father, who was now retired, came in to work. The first thing he did was make new signs for the store's glass-enclosed deli case by writing the name of each food in all capital letters. Seven hours later, one of the clerks looked inside the deli case and screamed in horror. The new sign for the crab salad read, CRAP SALAD. "No *wonder* we haven't sold any crab salad all day!" she said.

Call it human nature, but most people don't double-check their hand-written work or their computer-typewritten work. Even when creating important documents like resumes. When I first began freelancing full time, I wrote resumes to earn extra cash. I ran an ad in my local newspaper that read, "A bad resume won't get you a better job. For a great resume, call (my phone number)." Boy, did I get some *bad* resumes. Job seekers who had mailed dozens of resumes and hadn't had any luck getting a single job interview called me and mailed resumes to me that were littered with typos. One man spelled his own name wrong. His last name was "Miller" and at the top of his resume, he had spelled it with three ls, "Milller." Another man was sending out resumes that listed as his mailing address an apartment he had lived in two years ago. Hmm. Maybe that's why he hadn't received any reply letters. Then there was the guy who got his own job title wrong. He was a pre-press technician at a printing company, and he listed his current job at the top of his resume as "Stripper." He wasn't a male stripper, but that's probably what the human resources managers who glanced at his resume thought, right before they threw it away.

Newspapers are notorious for publishing funny errors. In a review of the Star Wars movie, "Attack of the Clones," a *Seattle Post-Intelligence* movie critic wrote, "The press was not given an advance peak" at the film. I think he wanted a "peek" at the movie before reviewing it. An Associated Press headline in the *Idaho Statesman* read, "Charge dismissed in wreckless-flying case." An airline pilot was brought on charges for *not* wrecking the plane? I don't think so. A *New York Times* article which announced that Walter Isaacson, the editorial director of Time, Inc., was named the new head of CNN, stated that Isaacson "will take the reigns" instead of "will take the reins" of the prestigious news gathering organization. Sounds like a real dictator. And a restaurant review in the *Jackson Citizen-Patriot* said, "a piano player was tinkling in the background." He was probably tickling the piano keys softly, but the review made it sound like something the health department should investigate.

Perhaps because information is so easy to post on the Internet nowadays, many typos and errors can be found online. A Yahoo! news headline announced, "U.S. Clams to Have Linked Attack Suspects to bin Laden." Mollusks are gathering new intelligence about the war on terrorism? Let's use people instead. I saw a job wanted posting on an employment Web site from a "stay-at-mom" who wanted to find work she could do in her home. She probably won't get any proofreading offers. And an Internet advertising banner that touted an online intelligence test was headlined, "Intelleginece Test." Not even close.

No one is perfect, not even the big-time editors of national magazines. I received a hand-written note from the editor of a national writing magazine after sending her a query letter for an article idea I titled, "Seven Things a Freelance Writer Should Never Say." In her note, she thanked me for the "7 things a writter should never say" query and said she would keep it under consideration. The editor of a writing magazine actually misspelled the word "writer."

Even if all the words are spelled correctly, a writer can make a grammar gaffe simply by misplacing a phrase in a sentence. An Associated Press report sent out on the wire service to newspapers across the nation described an accident as follows: "A short time later, 16 people were injured when Grubman backed into a crowd waiting to enter the club at high speed." Now I don't know if those people really were planning to run into the nightclub at high speed — were they *really* thirsty? — but the report suggests it, nonetheless.

A grammer gaffe in my local newspaper, the *Kalamazoo Gazette*, helped promote my freelance writing career. My husband, Dale, was reading the sports section, and suddenly he sat upright in his chair and said, "You're in Jack Moss's column today!" The sports editor's column profiled an article I had written for a regional business news publication, *Business Direct Weekly*. Jack Moss knew the man I had interviewed — the owner of a small, family-owned bank — and his weekly column included an interesting sports-related anecdote about this banker. But one sentence in the column contained phrases that were out of order, which made it sound as if I, not the bank, was successful. It read, "The bank has assets of $85 million, notes Nancie Hudson of BDW, who authored the story, and obviously is successful."

One of the most embarrassing errors a publication can make is spelling "public affairs" without an l. During the three and a half years that I worked in the public affairs department of a large oil company, it was my responsibility to make sure that every single piece of paper that left our department did not misspell the word public. I found that error many times, and we were always able to correct it before sending out the press release or news bulletin. So I had to laugh when years later I read an announcement on the front page of a chamber of commerce magazine that invited chamber members to volunteer for a new "pubic affairs committee" that was being formed. I wonder how many people volunteered for *that*.

Never misspelling a word again has been a priority of mine ever since my third-grade spelling bee. This was my chance to shine in front of my classmates, because I was a voracious reader of books. Every week I walked to the local library and checked out as many books as I could carry home, and I actually read every book before returning it, so my vocabulary was much more comprehensive than those of the other kids. One by one, the other kids misspelled words and were sent in shame to the back of the classroom to watch the nail-biting drama unfold. The contest got down to me and Danny, the smartest boy in the class. Then the teacher asked me to spell the word, "whistle." I was so excited that I knew about the silent "h" and therefore was sure to win the spelling bee that instead of slowly and carefully writing it on the blackboard, I hurriedly wrote, "whistel." Turning around, I expected the teacher to triumphantly announce, "Correct!" Instead, she announced, "Wrong!" Then everyone in the classroom watched as she raised Danny's arm in victory and announced, "Danny is the winner!" Danny beamed with pride, the class cheered, and I stood at the blackboard, wanting to disappear in a puff of smoke like Barbara Eden on "I Dream of Jeannie." Then after class, the teacher said to me privately, "Nancie, I thought you *knew* how to spell whistle. You never misspell *any* words, so I thought *you* would win." *That* made me feel even worse!

I think many human errors are caused by a combination of excitement and haste. For example, right after my husband, Dale, and I moved to Traverse City, Michigan many years ago, I saw a help wanted ad in the *Traverse City Record-Eagle* for a marketing position I was uniquely qualified for. My resume was ready, so I sat down at my word processor, typed what I thought was a perfect cover letter, signed it, and dropped the letter and resume into the mailbox in front of our apartment. After the mailman came, emptied the mailbox and drove away, Dale looked at my file copy of the letter and said, "You misspelled the word peninsula!" Sure enough, I had spelled it like Pennsylvania, with two ns, as in "penninsula." That was important, because the name of the company began with the word peninsula. So I had misspelled the company's name! Needless to say, they never called me in for an interview.

Years later I found out that if you misspell a word in an important letter and act quickly, you can actually get it back from the post office. I had just quit my job to become a full-time freelance writer, and I was anxious to write and sell articles to magazines, so when during a visit to my dentist I saw a press release about gum disease being linked to heart disease, I decided to pitch an idea for a feature article about it to a national health news magazine. Only trouble was, my hastily-prepared query letter misspelled the scientific name for gum disease, "periodontitus." I spelled it like it's pronounced, "peridontitus." What editor in his or her right mind would assign an article to a freelance writer who can't properly spell the topic? My mailman had already picked up the outgoing mail from our mailbox, so I called our local post office for help. The nice woman there said that when our carrier came back, she would ask him to retrieve it from his outgoing mail bag. Meanwhile, I drove over to the post office as fast as I could without getting a speeding ticket. When I walked into the post office and said I was the freelance writer who had called because she misspelled a word in an important letter and needed it back, my mail carrier and all the other postal workers laughed out loud. I became known as the local writer who can't spell, but I got the letter back!

Sometimes humans make mistakes because we get overwhelmed. That was certainly the case when I planned a 25th wedding anniversary party for my dad and step-mom, Stu and Betty. For nine months I planned this gala, and I wanted every detail of the party to be perfect — the hall, the decorations, the photographer, the disc jockey, the wedding cake, and so on. I kept a master checklist, and as soon as my step-sister or my brother or one of my parents' friends volunteered to do something such as bring a coffeemaker or hand-make centerpieces for the banquet tables, I checked it off the master list. I volunteered to handle the invitations, and I created them on my computer and printed them on elegantly-shaped white invitation card stock. Inside each invitation was a small map to the rental hall which I had hand-drawn and photocopied. But the night before the big party as Dale and I were relaxing and feeling as if we had everything under control, I looked at the hand-drawn map again and noticed that I forgotten to write in the name of the main street on which the hall was located! All the guests figured out which street it was and made it to the party, but no one in my family trusts me to draw maps anymore.

Most people assume that highway road signs are correct, but even our government makes mistakes. Two years ago, contractors hired by the Michigan Department of Transportation to do a huge road construction project on U.S. 131 discovered that two highway exits had been identified incorrectly for the past 10 years — exit 77 is actually 76 miles from the Indiana border, and exit 76 is 77 miles from the state line. Thinking they were doing a good thing, these contractors changed all the exit ramp signs for exit 76 to exit 77 and all the signs for exit 77 to exit 76. As a result, all the regular travelers on U.S. 131 — families, commuters and big-rig truck drivers that drive from Michigan to Florida and back — drove onto the exit ramp identified as exit 76 looking for their favorite pit-stop, the Exit 76 Truck Plaza, where they routinely stop for fuel, food, coffee and a much-needed bathroom break, and found themselves at a barren country crossroads they had never seen before! It was especially troublesome for the big-rig truck drivers, as the "new" exit 76 interchange didn't have a parking lot large enough for the drivers to turn their trucks around. The Michigan Department of Transportation received so many complaints about the new signs that it ordered contractors to change all the exit signage back to the way it was. Exit 76 is once again at 76th Street, where the Exit 76 Truck Plaza awaits road-weary travelers 24 hours a day. It's 77 miles from the Indiana border, but who's counting?

# Chapter 3

# Let's Make a Deal

A new car! That was the American dream when I was growing up, and television game show hosts like Monty Hall on "Let's Make a Deal" handed out the keys to new cars practically every weekday on TV. The lucky winner would jump up and down, shed tears of joy and give Monty Hall a big bear hug, wrinkling and/or smearing makeup on his previously perfect suit.

Today you don't see very many Americans winning new cars, because now people who go on TV game shows usually win money. So even if you are lucky enough to win money, you still have to go out and buy your own new car. That is, you have to make a deal.

Buying a car begins with the test drive. This is where you, the customer, drive a car, truck or van that you've never driven before, so you don't know where the controls are or, for that matter, how they work. Sure, while you're driving down the road you probably will be able to figure out how to turn the left turn signal on, but if it suddenly starts raining, will you be able to figure out how to turn on the windshield wipers *before* the water-streaked windshield completely obscures your vision of the road ahead, causing you to crash this new car into the SUV you're in traffic behind?

That's simple, you say, just figure out how to work all the buttons, knobs and levers before you pull out of the dealership parking lot. While that sounds good in theory, it's not what usually happens. The excitement of driving a new car — enhanced, of course, by that intoxicating new car smell — makes most people so anxious that they just take off. Then, of course, they have to figure out how to work the critical buttons, knobs and levers in moving traffic, sandwiched between a garbage truck and a city bus.

The trouble with the test drive is, either the salesman rides along, or he doesn't. Either way, you'll wish the opposite were happening. If he doesn't ride along — just hands you the car keys and watches you drive out of the dealership parking lot — you don't have anyone in the next seat who can answer your impromptu questions, such as, "Why is the dashboard suddenly beeping, and how do I make it stop?" And you don't have a navigator, so after driving off onto a road you've never been on before and then making two or three turns, you have to call the salesman on your cell phone and admit that you need directions back to the dealership.

If the salesman rides along, you're nervous because your nose is a few inches from his nose, and you don't really know him well enough to be nose to nose. The tension can be uncomfortable, so many salesmen talk to their customers during the test drive. That would be fine, if only they would limit their comments to things the driver actually wanted to know, such as how to turn on the windshield wipers or how to make the dashboard stop beeping.

Actually, I feel sorry for the new car salesman who has to ride along on the test drive, because he's a captive prisoner who never knows what kind of driver each customer will be. While interviewing new car salesmen for an article about the test drive, I heard several stories about customers who drove like they were in the Indianapolis 500 so they could test the vehicle's performance. "I had one gentleman who was doing 70 miles per hour on the entrance ramp to the highway, and that was very scary," one salesman told me. "What did you say to him?" I asked. "There wasn't too much I could say," he replied. "I was too busy hanging on for my life."

Another salesman told me that some customers drive normally until they get onto the highway and then, while going 70 or 75 miles per hour, they start slamming the steering wheel from left to right to see how the car handles. Then there are customers who suddenly panic, stop the car in the middle of a busy four-lane road, get out of the car and tell the salesman they want *him* to drive back to the dealership.

One salesman I interviewed told me that he doesn't make any sales pitches to the customer during the test drive. "When they are driving the vehicle, they have their own questions," he said. "If you're driving a vehicle down the road, do *you* want somebody talking to *you*?"

Based on this 10-minute test drive, you're supposed to be able to decide whether you want to drive this car for the next four, five or 10 years. But if you *do* decide that you love this car, don't tell that to the salesman. I've actually been told that by more than one new car salesman. You've got to play it cool, like you've got lots of options, so your salesman will work really hard to make you happy. Kind of like dating, really.

So you've decided that you *do* want to buy this car, and now you're in the salesman's office, sitting across the desk from him. Suddenly the atmosphere changes. He's no longer trying to impress *you*, because he knows that you want to buy the car you just test drove. You're trying to impress *him* that you have good credit and are able to afford making 60 monthly payments on this car over the next five years. You have to fill out the application, show your driver's license and answer questions about your income and debt, which most people regard as none of anyone else's business. But you tell all, in the hopes of driving away this new car.

If you're lucky, you'll sit in the salesman's office for one or two hours and then be approved. But one time I sat in a salesman's office for four hours, thrilled because I expected to drive home in a new car, and then was not approved. *Ouch.* What works best, I've discovered after many years, is to give the salesman all of the information to evaluate your financial situation and then go home and wait by the phone. Rest assured, he will call you as soon as he gets the news from his finance manager whether or not you have been approved. If you are, you can go back to the dealership the same day or the next day to take delivery of the vehicle, which will have been detailed — that means cleaned up, with a full tank of gas — instead of waiting in his office to be approved and then waiting while the service department details the vehicle. Unless, of course, you enjoy being in this dealership so much that you *want* to spend hours waiting there. After all, they *do* have a candy machine and free coffee.

Now you're driving your new car out of the dealership parking lot. Yippee! You drive to a friend's house to show them the new car. Everyone's happy for you. You spend the rest of the day celebrating your new purchase, thinking that the rest of your life will be perfect.

The next day an entirely different type of stress sets in — the aftershock of buying a new car. One reason this happens is most people don't sit right down and read the

505-page owner's manual for their new car. I remember driving home in one new car, turning it off, and then noticing a blinking red light on the dashboard. "What's that for?" I asked my husband. "I don't know," he replied, "but if it keeps doing it, it might run down the battery." After flipping through the owner's manual to no avail, I called the salesman and asked in a panicky voice what we did wrong and how could we make the red blinking light stop blinking. He calmly explained that it's supposed to blink whenever the car is off, because it's an anti-theft indicator, and it won't run down the battery. *Oh.*

Yes, understanding one's new car is very important. Years ago my dad was in a new car dealership looking at vehicles when a woman drove up and complained to the salesman that the new car she had bought one month earlier was getting terrible gas mileage, only eight or nine miles per gallon. "That's strange," the salesman said. "It's supposed to get much higher gas mileage." Then he looked into the car and noticed that the choke button, the knob-like button that regulated the flow of gasoline in older cars, was pulled out all the way. "Do you always drive around with that button pulled out?" he asked. "Yes," she replied. "That's the button I hang my purse on."

After buying a new car, many people also experience a heightened fear of getting into an accident. Some of that fear is logical, because today's drivers can be pretty reckless, especially on Interstate highways, but some of it is just the long-held belief in Murphy's Law: Anything that can go wrong, will. My dad told me that right after buying his first new car, he was terrified of getting into an accident. Finally one day while making a right-hand turn onto a busy street, he pulled out in front of an oncoming car, and the car dented the left front fender of dad's previously perfect car. But he said he was actually relieved, because from that point on, he didn't have to protect a perfect car, and he could relax and enjoy driving it.

My Dutch grandfather was a banker who bought a new car every two years, and he had a proven method for getting the vehicle he wanted at the price he wanted to pay. He would go to a dealership, talk with a salesman, test drive a car, and then go home. He did this every day for six consecutive days, always talking to the same salesman at the same dealership about the same car. By the sixth day, the salesman would become so anxious to sell the car and get his sales commission that he would agree to the lower price Grandpa VanderStel wanted to pay.

That worked for Grandpa VanderStel back in the 1950s, but I wouldn't dare try it today. If you keep coming back every day, the salesman might think you have a crush on him, and he might ask you out, which would be especially awkward if you're married. He might lose patience and say something like, "Come on, fish or cut bait." Or at the very worst, the general manager of the dealership might think you're casing the joint, planning to rob them, and call the local police. Then you'd have some explaining to do.

Overall, buying a new car is one of the most exciting, albeit stressful, experiences a person can go through. But if you can get through it and in the end, be happy with the car and the price you paid for it — *that* is the real American dream.

# Chapter 4

# Europe on $5 a Day

When I was 12, my mom took me on a six-week summer vacation through five European countries. She had read a book entitled: *Europe on $5 a Day*, and trusting that everything in this book was *true*, that a person actually could survive in Europe on only $5 a day, she saved money for two years so we could go on this ambitious adventure. Now most Americans went to Europe as part of an organized tour, where every detail of your trip was planned — every sightseeing stop was timed to the minute, and every meal was served in accordance with a pre-planned menu. That would be too *boring*, mom said. So off we went, a mother and daughter alone. We didn't speak any European languages, and we didn't have any credit cards. American tourists without a tour guide and without a clue on a budget of $5 per person per day.

With joy in my heart, new socks on my feet and way too much camera film in my suitcase, I boarded the plane with mom in Detroit and we flew to Amsterdam. Amsterdam was a picturesque city of historic brick buildings with a flower-filled window box adorning almost every window in sight. And it was clean, very clean. The first morning when I woke up and looked out the window of the five-story hostel where we were staying, I saw a Dutch woman scrubbing the sidewalk using soap, water and a push broom. I had heard about this tradition from my Dutch grandparents, who both emigrated from the Netherlands to Grand Rapids, Michigan when they were only 19 years old. I grabbed my camera, scampered down the stairs and ran out to the sidewalk. "May I take your picture?" I asked her. She spoke very little

English but understood that I wanted to take her picture, and she nodded and posed with a big smile on her face. She didn't understand *why* I wanted to get a picture of her scrubbing the sidewalk, because it was just a chore she and other Dutch property owners did every week. You know how American neighbors compete to have the best-looking lawn? In Amsterdam, the coolest house on the block is the one with the cleanest sidewalk.

All the Dutch people were friendly and extremely gracious. During our two-week stay in Amsterdam, mom and I often went to Vondel Park, a large city park that has a river running through it and is meticulously landscaped with trees, shrubbery and flowers. It was a relaxed, happy place where couples sat on park benches holding hands, children played with toy boats on the river, and a constant stream of people of all ages strolled the paved pathways. We would stop at a corner deli, buy a few slices of bread and cheese and some fruit for an inexpensive lunch, and eat it in the park. Mom was always ready to try something new, and one day she bought a bottle of some mysterious beverage that didn't have a twist-off cap. So as we sat on our favorite park bench eating, she couldn't get her beverage open. Frustrated, she began asking people who were walking by if they had a bottle opener. Turns out, Dutch people don't normally carry around bottle openers. But one well-dressed gentleman had a pocket knife, and he sat down and worked on opening that bottle cap with it until his hand bled. "There you are, maam," he proudly announced after he had pried the troublesome cap off. We were awed by this man's kindness, and mom thanked him profusely. Then he walked away smiling and waving, and we never saw him again. But I'll bet there's still a well-dressed gentleman who always carries a bottle opener whenever he walks through the park, just in case someone needs one. That's how nice the Dutch people are.

One day at Vondel Park we saw a gathering of people standing around the large gazebo and investigated. The crowd was watching a group of Hare Krishnas, men with shaved heads wearing nothing but orange togas and sandals. They danced around and sang their religious chanting song, which was mesmerizing. They passed around bowls of white snack balls that tasted very sweet, like rice and sugar. Then after they had lulled us into submission, they passed around a bowl for donations. I noticed that other children were climbing the gazebo walls to get a closer look, so I did, too. That's when I saw the television camera. A local news team was covering the event. Later that day when mom and I were eating dinner with other guests in the dining room of our hostel, we saw the report on TV. "Look, that's Nancie!" mom said, and everyone looked up at the TV just in time to see the camera zoom in on my face. I had made my television debut in Europe, quite a thrill for a 12-year-old American girl. But that irritating, redundant Hare Krishna song stuck in my head for *years*.

Staying at a hostel in Amsterdam is very inexpensive, so if you're on a budget and not looking for lodging frills, it's the best way to stretch your travel dollar. There is no elevator and there are no bell boys, so you have to carry your suitcases up several flights of stairs. The guest rooms have a window, but they are very small bedrooms that don't include a bathroom. To use the bathroom, you have to stand in line to use the bathroom at the end of the hall on each floor. Every night, mom and I stood in line in our bathrobes in the hallway with other guests, waiting our turn to take baths, brush our teeth and get ready for bed. It *was* a good way to get acquainted with the other guests, because when you have to stand in line to use the bathroom, the silence gets pretty awkward. Plus, your conversation drowns out those embarrassing bathroom noises other guests are making in there. But the hostel did serve a free breakfast in the dining room, one soft-boiled egg per person, a basket of freshly baked pastries and a pot of coffee. Every morning we rushed downstairs so we wouldn't miss out on the flaky croissant rolls, which were everyone's favorite. And for a nominal extra charge, you could eat a hot meal in the dining room at dinner time. For lunch, you were on your own.

Sightseeing in Amsterdam was fun and easy because they have a great public transportation system, the above-ground tram system. Trams are like clean buses that ride on rails throughout the city, and it's easy to hop on and off at will. We walked down the quaint sidestreets of the riverway canals. We observed the tall, narrow, historic buildings and the Dutch people riding their bicycles. If it was free, we did it. But if you go, do *not* go to the House of Anne Frank. I knew all about the diary of Anne Frank and couldn't wait to see the room at the top of the house where she and her family hid out from the Nazis. Ready to climb more stairs, we entered the house and looked around the first floor, which was like a museum, decorated with pictures of the Frank family, historic documents, and Dutch souvenirs. That was entertaining, for about five minutes. Then I asked when we were going to go upstairs. "You can't go *upstairs*," the woman said. "This building is too old to have hundreds of people climbing up those stairs every day. It wouldn't be safe." "So what's the *point* of seeing the house if you can't see the room upstairs?" I said loudly. Then mom suggested I buy a souvenir with my allowance so the nice Dutch lady wouldn't be mad.

After two weeks in Amsterdam, we checked out of the hostel and boarded the train for Paris. Getting around Europe was easy because mom had bought a Eurailpass for each of us, so we could board any train in Europe free of charge. And the trains were really clean and nice. They even had a dining car with white linen tablecloths. Traveling through the Netherlands, we saw the Dutch windmills harnessing wind power in the fields. On the way, the train went through Belgium, and we admired the neatly maintained farms and farmhouses. We entered France and marveled at the beauty of the French countryside. Then after arriving in Paris, we found our way to the hotel and were absolutely *thrilled* to discover that our room had a private bathroom! Aaah, the good life.

We didn't speak French, but we had an English to French pocket dictionary, and with that in hand, we struggled to communicate with the Parisians in their language. They *loved* that, because for two hundred years they've been dealing with American tourists who don't even try to speak French. So even if you mispronounce their language badly, they smile and emulate compassion and do everything they can to help you. The man who operated the street deli around the corner from our hotel helped us learn to pronounce a few basic French phrases so we could tell him what we wanted to eat. We bought a loaf of French bread, a few slices of cheese, a box of crackers and some fresh fruit and took them back to our hotel room. Because that's how you eat in Europe on only $5 a day.

The city of Paris was everything we expected and more. First, we visited the Eiffel Tower. We took the bus to where we thought it was and looked around but didn't see it because there are so many landmarks and trees in Paris that block one's view at street level. Then we saw a Parisian street vendor who was selling freshly-fried crepes. "We've *got* to try a French crepe!" mom said, so she splurged and bought two strawberry crepes for us. They were warm and buttery and delicious. "Where is the Eiffel Tower?" mom said to the vendor. "Tour Effel?" he replied, because that's what the French call it. He pointed in the direction we should walk, and as soon as we rounded the corner, we saw it. The Eiffel Tower was spectacular. Mere photographs cannot capture the feeling of looking up at its magnificent architecture. We went up to the first landing of the tower and saw all the landmarks in Paris from a bird's eye view. Now we knew where everything in Paris was. Now we were confident. Too confident. We got lost.

We knew our way around the heart of the city and were fine as long as we visited easy-to-find landmarks such as the ornately awesome Arch of Triumph and Notre Dame Cathedral, but being an artist, mom *had* to go see the artist colony at Mont Martre. Every day scores of French artists set up their easels on the sidewalks of the streets that surrounded the hilltop cathedral, and every day busloads of tourists watched them at work and bought their paintings. Mom was so excited that I think she chatted with every single artist there. No matter what they were painting, she loved it. We were so engrossed in the ambience of the artist colony that we lost track of time and missed the last bus that transported tourists back into the hotel district. The artists were packing up their easels and leaving. So we started walking down the hill. But the sidestreets didn't go straight down the hill, they went in all directions. We kept walking. The sun was going down, and the air was getting chilly. Then it started to rain. Lucky for us, mom had brought her umbrella. As we walked, we noticed that the streets were barren of pedestrians, but on every block, there was a woman in a trenchcoat standing by the curb, holding an umbrella, as if she were waiting for someone. Turns out, we were in Pigalle (pih-gahl'), the red light district of Paris. "Those are prostitutes," mom told me. "Don't look at them or smile at them." On and on we walked, past the French prostitutes, who stared at us. Just when it was getting really dark and our legs were getting tired, we recognized the name of a street and knew we were getting close to our hotel. Yippee! We found our way back to the hotel, where the nice French lady at the front desk who spoke English expressed concern that we hadn't returned earlier. "You got lost in *Pigalle*?" she said. "Why did you not take the *bus* back from Mont Martre?"

The next day we took the train into the French countryside to visit the little town of Nancy, which is 150 miles from Paris. It's a nice day trip, if you know when to get off the train. At every stop, the conductor would announce the name of the town over the intercom. Then as the train started up again, he would announce the name of the next few towns we were approaching. Mom and I were listening for "Nan-see" as Americans pronounce it, which rhymes with fancy. But the French pronounce it "Nah-see." So as the train sped toward Nancy, we weren't planning to get off. Then mom struck up a conversation with a good-looking French man and told him we were Americans who were going to visit the town she had named me after, Nan-see. "You mean Nah-see," he said. "That's the next stop!" We thanked him and got off the train just in time. Otherwise, we would have ended up in Switzerland.

Nancy was a small town, so it didn't take long for us to walk around and see everything there was to see — small buildings, small houses, a small church and a park that had golf-course quality green grass and a formal flower garden with every flower one could imagine growing neatly in rows according to size and height. We stretched out on the soft grass and basked in the warm sun, admiring the flower garden. Then we went to the pastry shop across the street from the park and each picked out one French pastry — which was really hard to do, because there were at least 50 different pastries to choose from. We took our pastries and beverages to the park and ate them while sitting on the grass. It was so beautiful and quiet that it seemed like paradise. Then mom took a picture of me in Nancy, France, and for the first time in my life, I was proud of my name. But the name didn't originate in France, I learned years later. The Nancy family crest can be traced back to Cornwall, England, and one of the first Nancys to emigrate to the United States was a woman named Nancy Nance who arrived in Philadelphia in 1820. *Her* parents certainly had a sense of humor.

Twice during our Paris vacation we ate in a Parisian restaurant, which is considerably less enjoyable if you're living on $5 a day. The first time, we were walking down the famous shopping boulevard, the Champs Elysee, and mom said she had *always wanted* to eat in a French restaurant that overlooks the Champs Elysee. It must be expensive, mom said, so we'll just order soup. We climbed the stairs to this elegant restaurant and were seated at a table that provided a panoramic view of the boulevard. Then the French waiter brought our menus, and we saw the prices. Yikes! We didn't have *that* many francs. All we could afford was one piece of pie and one cup of coffee. So that's what we ordered. The waiter rolled his eyes and brought them to our table.

The second time we ate in a French restaurant, mom chose a small restaurant on a sidestreet in a residential neighborhood near the Champs Elysee, where she figured the prices must be lower. The prices were lower, but the menu was written in French — not in both French and

English, as the menus at the elegant restaurant had been — and we had left our English to French pocket dictionary in our hotel room. Not having a clue what we were ordering because the French waitress spoke no English, we each pointed to a low-priced item on the menu and then waited to see what we got. Mine was French onion soup, which I hated. Mom's was split pea soup, which I also hated. So as I watched mom eat both bowls of soup, I realized how important a decision can be. In France if you don't speak French and make the wrong decision when ordering food, you go hungry until you get back to your hotel room and eat bread and cheese. That is, if you're living on $5 a day.

Mom and I didn't want to leave Paris after our seven-day vacation there, because there was still so much to see. We hadn't even seen the world-famous Louvre art museum yet. But a family in Switzerland was expecting us to visit them, so we checked out of our comfortable hotel room with the private bathroom and took the train to Zurich. As the train sped through the French countryside, we sat in the formal dining car with the white linen tablecloths, china plates, crystal goblets and real silverware and were served an elegant lunch of beef tips in brown gravy, herbed potatoes, French-style green beans in butter sauce, and French bread. Mom said we could splurge because we didn't have to pay for a hotel room that night. And it was worth it, because eating in the formal dining car made us feel like royalty. Then after the train entered Switzerland, we saw the Swiss Alps for the first time. The bright sun illuminated every curve of their snow-capped splendor. It was breathtakingly beautiful.

The Swiss family picked us up at the Zurich train station. We had been matched with them because they also had a 12-year-old daughter, and they were very excited to be entertaining Americans. They drove us to their Swiss chalet, which was built on the side of a steep hill. The front of the chalet was a wall of windows that overlooked a green valley and beyond the valley, a mountain. We all gathered around the stone fireplace in the living room and grinned at each other. The only trouble was, we didn't speak either of the languages they spoke, Swiss and German, and they didn't speak any English. For a born communicator like me, it was very frustrating. Here I was, face to face with a Swiss girl my age, wanting to ask her about all the details of her daily life and tell her about mine, and we couldn't understand a word the other said. Why didn't we bring an English to Swiss pocket dictionary? *That* would have been helpful. But the Swiss mom and daughter cooked a huge pot of something that tasted like beef stew — I *hope* it was beef — and we gathered around the big wooden dining room table and ate the mysterious stew and bread until our bellies were stuffed. That night mom slept on the living room couch, and I bunked with their daughter in her loft bedroom, which was small but had two built-in, kid-size beds with soft feather pillows and thick, white, down comforters. Falling asleep in that bed, I felt like Heidi, the Swiss mountain girl in the children's storybooks. All I needed was a walking stick and a pet mountain goat.

After the Swiss family drove us back into Zurich, we checked into our hotel there. It was a modern, 10-story hotel, and our guest room was small but it had a private bathroom with a huge, walk-in shower. Now I had never taken a shower before in my life, so I couldn't *wait* to try to get clean standing up instead of soaking in my own dirt. Wearing my bathing cap to keep my hair dry, I got into the shower. Aaah. Our first day in Zurich, I showered three times. So I must have been the cleanest tourist there.

But when my fingers started to prune up, mom said I had showered enough for one day.

The next day mom said we were going to the beach at an Alpine lake. We waited for the bus in front of our hotel and rode it to the beach at Lake Zurich. The lake was small but deep, and its sapphire blue water shimmered in the sunlight. Beyond the lake was a small snow-capped mountain. Wow! Pretty enough to be on a postcard. We walked onto the beach, wanting to get as close to the water as possible, and saw an empty span of beach right behind two Swiss women who were sitting on beach towels facing the water. "Here's a good spot," mom announced, and we spread out our towels, pulled off our tops and shorts, revealing our bathing suits underneath, and sat down to enjoy the scenery. The two women were talking very fast in another language, but otherwise, the beach was quiet. A peaceful setting. Then the two women in front of us stopped talking and laid back on their towels. That's when mom and I noticed that they weren't wearing any bathing suit tops! Their bare, suntanned breasts were only four feet away. Mom and I looked at each other with our mouths open in shock. Then we wanted to laugh, but we had to stifle our laughter because the beach was so quiet. "Don't stare," mom whispered to me, but it was pretty hard not to. I had *never* seen anything like this back home on the beach at Lake Michigan. But as Americans visiting another country, we had to be polite. So mom and I tried not to stare at them and engaged in casual conversation, such as, "Wasn't that Swiss chalet beautiful?" and "Boy, I wish we had a shower back home," when we wanted to say, "Can you *believe* those women aren't wearing any tops on a public beach?" and "What if their breasts get sunburnt? Wouldn't *that* be painful?"

We were glad we had gone to the beach that day, because it rained every day for the rest of our stay in Zurich. Mom re-read her travel book, and I took lots of showers. Then it was time to check out and take the train to Munich, Germany. There we stayed in a small hotel room that didn't have a shower, but it did have a private bathroom. Munich was a pretty city with lots of parks, and the weather was sunny and comfortably warm. We walked through the parks, took pictures of the colorful flower gardens, and read the inscriptions on all the war memorial monuments and statues. But we were the only people in the parks. Where were all the German people? We found them when we discovered the beer gardens. I think that's where the Germans spent their leisure time every day, because the beer gardens were always busy. Mom had a great time at the beer gardens. Everyone but me seemed to be having a *great* time, talking and laughing and singing German songs loudly as street musicians entertained for tips. Then again, everyone else was quaffing a huge mug of beer, and I was drinking a glass of soda. Sensing that I wasn't having nearly as much fun as she was, mom promised to take me shopping the next day.

Shopping in Germany? On only $5 a day? It was our last day in Germany, and mom surprised me by revealing that she had set aside money in her checking account back home to buy each of us a traditional German costume. We took the train across the German countryside to a small town where there was a quaint, historic-themed shopping village. All the German people who worked in the village wore traditional German costumes, and we found a small shop that sold the costumes. The owner of the shop was a friendly German woman who spoke English, so mom introduced us and told her that we had come all the way from America to buy authentic German peasant blouses and frocks! We spent the next hour trying on blouses and frocks until each of us found an ensemble that fit perfectly. We both chose short-sleeved, lace-trimmed white peasant blouses, Mom chose a red frock that was decorated with colorful embroidery, and the frock I chose was yellow-and-white checkered, the cutest little jumper I had ever seen. Looking into the mirror together, we were so happy and felt so pretty that mom started to dance to the German folk music that was playing in the shop. The German lady was already in costume, so she joined in the dance. The three of us held hands and danced in a circle. Everything seemed magical until we changed back into our regular clothing and went to the cash register to pay for the costumes. "Oh, *no*," mom said. "I forgot to put my checkbook in my purse. It's back at the hotel in Munich. I guess we can't buy the costumes after all, because tomorrow we can't come back here — we have to take the train to Vienna." Seeing the disappointment on our faces, the German lady who owned the shop said she would trust mom to mail a check to her when we got back to Munich. She wrote out the mailing address for her shop, gave it to mom and let us leave the store with the costumes. She said that we had honest faces, but I think she realized that no one would travel all the way from America to Germany just to steal German peasant blouses and frocks!

The next jaunt of our vacation in Vienna, Austria was awful, even though we stayed in a nice hostel where we had a large room with a private bathroom, because it rained every day for five days. On the first day, we tried to sightsee anyway and got soaked even though we were under mom's umbrella. So we hibernated in our spacious guest room at the hostel, hoping that the weather the next day would be nice. On the fourth day when it was raining again, I got antsy and complained that I was bored. "Let's change the furniture around!" mom said, because that's what we did back home on rainy days. We had a ball rearranging the couch, table, chairs, and beds to create a new interior design in our room. When we had finished, we sat down on the couch and admired our new setting. Then came a knock at the door. "What *are* you doing in there?" the Austrian woman who ran our hostel demanded to know. "What's all that noise?" When we let her in, she was horrified. Then she not only moved everything in the room back the way it had been, she *scolded* us as she did it. Mom wasn't accustomed to being scolded like a child, and I could tell that she no longer liked this Austrian woman. We were very glad that we were planning to leave Vienna the next day. Later that afternoon, the Austrian woman knocked on our door again. We both jumped, afraid we were going to be scolded again. But she was just delivering a letter to us from my brother back in Michigan. He was taking care of my dog, Pepsi, while we were gone, and the letter announced the news that Pepsi had given birth to a litter of six adorable little puppies! And we had missed it! Suddenly all we could think about was getting back home.

As we traveled through Europe, we met lots of other travelers, mostly married European couples who were on vacation or "on holiday" as they say. Whenever we told them that the last stop on our self-planned itinerary was Rome, Italy, they advised us not to go there. Rome was a romantic place for couples, they said, but it wasn't an ideal travel destination for families. Maybe we shouldn't go there, mom said. We pondered our next move. Neither of us wanted to go to another new place, and we could spend our last week in Amsterdam, Paris, Zurich or Munich. I voted for Amsterdam, and mom said she wanted to go back to Amsterdam, too. The city was so clean and beautiful, the people were so friendly and nice, and we loved Vondel

Park. Mom called the Dutch hostel where we had spent the first two weeks of our vacation, and they *did* have a guest room available for the next seven days! So the next day we took the train all the way back to Amsterdam and checked back into the hostel where you had to stand in line to use the bathroom at the end of the hall on each floor. But we were so happy to see the friendly Dutch lady who ran the hostel and be served the free flaky croissants each morning in the dining room and *not* encounter any more surprises that we thoroughly enjoyed our last week in Europe. We went back to Vondel Park and all our favorite places in Amsterdam. We did *not*, however, go back to the House of Anne Frank.

Visiting Europe for six weeks during the summer of 1973 was an eye-opening experience, and I'm not just referring to the topless women on the Swiss beach. Seeing and meeting all those different types of people and observing their cultures was a real-life education for me. But after we got back home, I kept thinking that if only Mom and I *had* been able to speak their languages, we might have been able to avoid making tourist mistakes, such as ordering soup that you hate.

However, the next summer my brother proved that an American tourist *can* get into trouble in Europe even if he *does* speak the language. After hearing about our adventures, Steve decided to go to France for his senior trip in college. He spoke French because he had studied French at the university. With 29 other college seniors and his French professor, he went on a two-week trip that included a visit to a medieval castle in the French countryside, Chinon Castle. Joan of Arc received her armies from King Louis XIV there, and King Richard the Lionheart died there after being wounded in battle. The group was led on a tour of the castle that ended shortly before 12 noon, and the tour guide said they could take a few minutes to look around on their own. Steve was so awed by the fact that he was in a *real* medieval castle that he didn't hear the tour guide say it was time for lunch. At 12:30, he noticed that everyone else was gone. He tried to push open the 18-foot-tall wooden doors in the castle's entrance, but the doors were now locked. He was locked inside the castle alone!

Steve had brought a sack lunch with him, so he climbed the stairs up to the castle's rooftop and up into the turret — the lookout tower — and had a private picnic, laughing about this unexpected turn of events and marveling at the scenic view. From the turret, you could see everything for 10 miles. Then he wandered through the castle, from the rooftop to the great hall to the dungeon. Being in the castle alone was very eerie, Steve said. He could feel the spirits of all the people who had lived and died there, particularly when he stood in the great hall and in the bedroom where King Richard the Lionheart had died. An hour passed, and still no one came back for him. Steve didn't know that the French take a two-hour lunch every day. The next tour wasn't until 2 o'clock. So he was alone in the castle for two hours. Creepy.

Many tourists visit medieval castles hoping to see a ghost, and back then, Steve looked medieval. He had long, red, shoulder-length hair and a big, bushy red beard and he was wearing old, drab-colored clothing. At 2 o'clock when the castle's huge wooden doors were unlocked and opened, the first few tourists that stepped inside were expecting to enter an empty castle and instead, saw Steve walking toward them. "You should have *seen* them," Steve said, laughing. "They jumped a mile high. They thought I was a *ghost!*"

# Chapter 5

# Truth Be Told

Today's job applicants tell the truth when they should lie and lie when they should tell the truth, according to the manager of a large luxury hotel. "They just blow me away by the fact that they're brutally honest," she said. She asks them, "How many times is it okay to be late for work in a month?" and they say, "One or two." "In my mind," she told me, "the answer should always be that you shouldn't be late for work at all." Job seekers also admit to her that they can't come to work on time, that they're not organized, or that their handwriting is horrible. "It's incredible," she said. "I actually interviewed a person for a position and he said, 'I really don't like working with other people.'"

People who apply for bell staff positions lie about their driving record, she said. Bell staff positions require adults who have a completely clean driving record, because the person will be driving the hotel's airport shuttle bus and driving guest vehicles in its valet parking service. "That's the most difficult obstacle I have," the hotel manager said. "People who come in and apply say they have a clean driving record, and then we'll run the background check, and they've got too many points, so we can't hire them."

Why are such people lying about their driving record — lie that can be disproven so easily — and telling the truth about their personal shortcomings and bad work habits — things they should keep to themselves? Because discerning when one should tell the truth and when one should not *can* be confusing.

My parents brainwashed me to *always* tell the truth. Yet sometimes they would tell me to lie, like when we were planning a practical joke or a surprise gift or a surprise party. But that can get a youngster into trouble. When my niece, Katy, was five years old, she lied to her father about sneaking over to another check-out lane in the grocery store to buy a bag of M&Ms while he was paying for groceries. Steve saw the bulge in her coat pocket and knew that she had just bought more candy, and he had just talked to her about not spending all her allowance on candy. Furious with her for lying, he gave her a spanking right in the store's main entrance. Tears streamed down her cheeks and people stared, but Katy didn't say a word. Then after they arrived back home, Steve told Katy's mother, Lisa, what had happened. To Steve's surprise, Lisa replied, "Katy bought those for *you*, as a surprise present for your birthday tomorrow. She knows M&Ms are your favorite."

Parents also tell their children to lie when they open a gift that they don't like, because you don't want to hurt the giver's feelings. They call those lies "little white lies." Those also can backfire, as in the case of the woman who received an ugly ceramic penguin from her aunt every Christmas for 20 years because as a child she told her aunt that she liked the first ugly ceramic penguin she received. So her aunt thought she collected ugly ceramic penguins. And she *did* end up with a collection of them.

With that in mind, is it okay to lie if the lie won't hurt anyone? Like the time a man I know had to lie in order to get a job that he needed to support his family. He had 15 years of experience and a master's degree and qualified for the position in every other way, but he didn't know how to use the company's computer software, and that was a requirement. So during the job interview, he said he knew how to use it, and before he started the new job, he went to the nearest university bookstore, bought the textbook for that computer software, and read the first few chapters. Then he carried the textbook to work in his briefcase, so he could refer to it as needed. And his employer never found out that he didn't know how to use it when he took the job, so no harm done, right?

Conversely, I worked for a boss that lied to me every day of the workweek, and I didn't find out about it until the first time he took a one-week vacation. He was the president of the company, and every day right before 3 o'clock, he would tell me that he was going to be working on a project for the next hour and didn't want to be disturbed for any reason. Like a British bobby, I guarded his office door until he emerged at 4 o'clock. So you can imagine my surprise when on the first day of his vacation, a Monday afternoon, the alarm on the alarm clock/radio in his office went off at 3:55 p.m. One other person heard it, a woman in the marketing department whose office was adjacent to his, and she and I investigated but couldn't figure out how to turn the alarm off, so we closed his office door and pondered what to do next. After five minutes, the alarm shut off automatically. Then we looked at each other and laughed, because we realized why his alarm had been set. Every day when he *said* he was working on a project, he was taking a secret nap on the couch in his office! And when the alarm sounded, he shut it off, straightened his tie, and casually emerged from his office. No *wonder* he always had so much energy at the end of the day! Not wanting to be fired, she and I never told him or anyone else in the company that we had discovered his secret. But from then on it was a private joke between us, because if he had remembered to reset his alarm clock so it wouldn't go off during his vacation, we probably never would have known the truth about his afternoon project time!

The rules for telling the truth in news reporting are absolutely clear — report the facts, and only the facts, in an objective way. Perhaps that's why I like journalism so much, because the rules are easy to follow. Yet some people have trouble grasping that concept. For example, on the first day of my first journalism class in college, a young girl raised her hand and asked the professor a question about our first assignment. After explaining to us the basics of the course, Professor Whitebird had asked us each to gather news on campus and write a short article. "Does it have to be *true*?" the girl asked. "*Yes*," he snapped. "Otherwise, this wouldn't be Journalism 101, it would be *Creative* Writing. That's down the hall in room 115, and anyone who wants to go down there should go right now." No one moved or said a word.

After class, I walked over to the campus administrator's office, introduced myself and asked what was new on campus. Turns out, the college had just installed new state-of-the-art physics equipment in the physics lab. The administrator gave me the physics professor's name and phone number, and I called him and arranged to meet him in the lab. The physics professor was very nice, but he had a heavy foreign accent, so I couldn't understand everything he said. Truth be told, after a 30-minute private tour of the lab, I still didn't have a clue what the new equipment was or what it did. How was I going to explain this new equipment in layman's terms if I didn't understand it myself?

Fortunately, we had met in the lab right before a lab class was to begin, so I hung around and observed the physics students using the equipment to conduct experiments and asked them questions. *Now* I understood, so I rushed home and typed up an article that announced and explained the new equipment using an analogy everyone could understand. Professor Whitebird liked the article so much that he suggested I give it to the campus administrator to send out to the media as a press release. The press release was a success, as my article appeared in the *Houston Chronicle* the following week. It also was a hit with another beginning journalism student who saw the article in the *Houston Chronicle*, copied it word for word, and turned it in as his own work! Professor Whitebird recognized it right away and gave him an F on the assignment. Because journalism requires telling the truth as *you* observe it. Copying someone else's news report is plagiarism.

The rules for telling the truth in news reporting are easy to understand, yet some people just don't comprehend how the journalism process works. Several years ago after I had conducted a 30-minute telephone interview with a small business owner about how and when his business started, what they sold and other pertinent facts, he called me back the next day and asked me, "Can you just say in your article that my business partner said all those things?" "No," I had to politely tell him, "then they wouldn't be quotes. A quote is an actual word-for-word record of something someone really said. We don't make those up."

When I wrote one of my first big feature articles for a Kalamazoo, Michigan-based business news publication, *Business Direct Weekly*, my research indicated that I was profiling a private foundation that allocated monies to organizations that promoted the health and well-being of dogs, cats and birds. So I wrote a fun story lead — the first sentence of a news article — that read, "A foundation for birds?" to snag the reader's interest. Only trouble was, the photographer who took the foundation administrator's picture told the news publication's editor, Michael Chevy Castranova, that they were only giving charitable contributions to organizations for dogs and cats, not birds. I was *very* disappointed when he called me and told me this news flash, because it meant they couldn't use the story lead I had written. "But it was such a *great* lead!" I said. "Sometimes the facts get in the way of those great leads," Castranova replied, laughing.

That's in the world of journalism. In real life, sometimes you *have* to lie in order to avoid hurting people's feelings. Because you can't tell your wife that her short new haircut makes her look like a beaver. You can't tell your boss that his custom-tailored brown business suit makes him look like a candy bar. And your neighbors would *not* want to hear that the mauve color they chose to repaint their house makes it look like a freshly-filleted salmon. Just keep your fingers crossed that you never open a gift and find an ugly ceramic penguin.

# Chapter 6

# Where Y'all From?

I never *planned* to move to Texas, I had planned to move to Florida. That's where everyone in Michigan went on vacation, so I figured it must be great. I was hoping to find a better job and a place to live where I wouldn't have to cover every inch of my skin just to go outside, as I had just survived one of the worst Michigan winters on record. I'll move down South, I thought. And my best friend, Shelly, had just moved to a small town in Florida with her husband, Ralph. So on a beautiful fall morning as my father watched in fear and disbelief, I set out for Florida with a person I barely knew. But Jack was a friend of a friend, he also wanted to move down South, and he had a dependable car. That was good enough for me.

When we arrived in Florida, the beaches were inviting, the weather was hot and sunny, and it seemed like heaven — until I looked for a job. Even though my qualifications were superb (exceptional clerical skills and three years of working for the same employer), the best job I could find was temporary clerical work that paid only minimum wage. But lucky for me, a lady in the office where I was temping had just received a letter from her sister who lived in Houston, and she had enclosed six pages of *Houston Chronicle* help wanted ads. Secretaries were in huge demand, and the starting salaries were twice as much as what I made back home! And Jack, who hadn't been able to find a job, said that his aunt Joan lived in Houston. So with a gallon of water and a container of buttered cornbread Shelly had thoughtfully prepared for our trip, Jack and I set out for Houston.

We had been driving all day and still had Florida beach sand between our toes, so as soon as we entered the Houston city limits, we started looking for a motel room where we could shower and get a good night's sleep before calling Jack's aunt. But every single hotel and motel was flashing a no vacancy sign. The only place we could find was a rest area on Interstate 10, and it was nearly full. Because hundreds of people were coming into Houston every day, looking for work. So we spent that first night sleeping in the front bucket seats of Jack's small car, without a gun, terrified that we would be easy prey for any criminal who happened to stop at that rest area. But everyone else was sleeping in their cars, too, so if anything happened, at least we would have witnesses to testify as to how and when we were brutally murdered, right?

We woke up early, about 6 a.m., stinky and stiff but happy to still be alive, and Jack called his aunt, Joan. She was thrilled that we were in town, as she hadn't seen Jack in 10 years, and she gave us directions to her home in southwest Houston.

That first week in Houston was an adventure. On Saturday night, Joan took us out to dinner at the best Tex-Mex restaurant in town, where we learned that the green sauce is hot, the red sauce is hotter, and eating jalapeno peppers makes your eyes water, your nose run, and your throat burn. It's a ritual of passage for all Northerners. The first thing Texans do is pop a jalapeno pepper into their mouths, say "Go ahead, try one," and then laugh at the newcomers' wimpy taste buds. But you forgive these friendly Texans, because they also order crispy bean and cheese nachos and marinated, grilled beef and chicken fajitas with all the fixins, more than enough for everyone at the table to share. And the atmosphere in the boldly decorated candlelit dining room is festive, with a roaming Mariachi band playing snappy Spanish songs on classical guitars. It's as if you're in Old Mexico (pronounced meh' hee ko). A real fiesta!

On Sunday night, Joan donned her red cowboy boots and insisted that I wear her white cowboy boots, and we all got dressed in our blue jeans and checkered shirts and went out to eat at a real Texas steakhouse. It was just like a saloon in America's Old West. Everything was wooden — the floors, the walls, the tables, the booths, even the menu, which was hand-painted on a wooden board in the foyer. Now Texans take their steak very, very seriously. In fact, Joan wouldn't let us order anything else, because it wouldn't be patriotic. "Y'all *have* to have the steak. Texas beef is the *best* beef in the world." And the 16-ounce slab of beef the waitress plunked down in front of me tasted like the best steak I had ever eaten. Then again, I hadn't eaten steak in two years.

Early Monday morning, I called an employment agency and went in for an interview. They tested my clerical skills, looked at my resume and the glowing letter of reference from my previous boss at the insurance company, and said, "Oh, you'll have no trouble finding a job here." And they were right. They sent me on three job interviews for high-paying secretarial positions and then called me on Thursday and said all three companies wanted to hire me. I could choose whichever job I wanted! I decided on the one where I had noticed that all the employees were happy, cheerful and relaxed. In the interests of not being sued, I'll call it Pumpmore Petroleum. Because no matter how much oil and gas the exploration department found and no matter how much oil and gas the production department pumped, the owner of the company always wanted more.

Pumpmore Petroleum was a worldwide oil and gas company that was run by a down-to-earth Texas oilman who wore three-piece business suits and cowboy boots to the office. He owned the company — no one could tell him not to. We were working in the company's headquarters, a 20-story high-rise office building with 800 employees. I was the secretary in a newly-formed public relations department on the tenth floor. Everyone in the public relations department had just been hired, and we were all from different parts of the United States. Our desks were empty, and there were no files. So on my first day, I got paid for reading the newspaper and smiling at everyone who got off the bank of elevators in front of my desk. I felt like Vanna White.

Working in Pumpmore Petroleum's public relations department was like being a cheerleader for a sports team that wins every game. (That was fun for me, as I had been a sixth-grade basketball cheerleader for a team that *lost* every game.) We would send out a news release, and like magic, an article about our oil or gas discovery would appear in both Houston daily newspapers and in all the regional oilfield publications. We created annual reports, a monthly employee newsletter, internal news bulletins — in short, all good news about the company. Which is why all the other employees liked us, I guess. Everyone likes to hear good news about their employer.

Living in a boomtown was exciting. There were so many people! Everywhere I went, people were smiling and in a great mood because everyone was making money. The check-out lines in every store were 10 or more people long, but it was an opportunity to chat. "Where are you from?" was the opening line, unless the person was a Texan. Then it was "Where y'all from?" "I'm from Kalamazoo," I said. "No, really," they said, laughing. "Where y'all from?" Nine out of 10 people had just relocated from Michigan, Ohio, Indiana or Illinois in search of work. And because there were so many job opportunities, everyone found a job.

The only problem was finding a place to live, because with the sudden population growth, there was a shortage of apartments. But I met a girl at a dinner party who had just signed a lease on a two-bedroom apartment and needed a roommate. And her apartment was across the street from the entrance to Joan's neighborhood. So I decided to move in with Tammy from Indiana. As nice as Joan was, it was time for me to leave. But she insisted that I keep her white cowboy boots, perhaps because I'd been wearing them for the past month. And she wouldn't let me pay her any money for letting me stay with her. I needed to save my money and buy a car, she said.

Joan was right. Everyone in Houston needed a car, because there was no reliable public transportation and the highway system was a concrete maze of 10-lane racetracks where speed limits were a joke. And it had to be a dependable car, because having car trouble on a highway could result in disaster. (This was before cell phones were invented.) Broken-down cars that had been stripped of batteries, radios, hub caps and tires were a common sight on Houston highways. A man I worked with at the oil company actually saw two men steal his car battery. He had run out of gas on U.S. 59, parked his car on the shoulder, walked to a gas station, bought a five-gallon container of gas and was walking back to his car when he saw up ahead that the hood of his car was open and two men were removing the battery. They got the battery, scampered down the hill, and ran away. A woman I knew was driving on a Houston freeway when the car behind her suddenly crashed into the back of her car, and all six of the men in the car climbed out and fled the scene. So when the police arrived on the scene, they found one woman and two wrecked cars. Hmm.

I had been car-pooling to and from work with Diana, a secretary at Pumpmore Petroleum, and Diana's older sister, Maria. The car-pool coordinator at Pumpmore Petroleum had set up the arrangement. I enjoyed riding with these personable Hispanic women, but every morning I worried that we would get into an accident on the highway because Maria would remove the hot rollers from her hair while driving in morning rush-hour traffic. Which, of course, required taking both hands off the steering wheel. Nervously I would chat with Diana about her latest date or newest dress while constantly ready to yell, "Stop!" if the driver in the car in front of us suddenly braked. So by the time we arrived at Pumpmore Petroleum, I was *wide* awake.

Even after paying Tammy for my half of that month's rent, I still had $1,000 in my checking account to use as a downpayment on a car. Thus I thought I would be able to march into a car dealership, pick out the car I wanted and drive away. So after work one day, I asked Maria to drop me off at a new car dealership on U.S. 59. I test drove a new sportscar and tried to buy it, but the salesman told me I couldn't qualify because I had no credit history, I had only been working at my job for a month, and I was from another state. OK, I said, I'll take the compact car. More waiting. Hours later, he informed me that I couldn't qualify for *any* car without a co-signer. Meekly I had to call Tammy and ask her to please come and pick me up.

The next day after work, I asked Maria to drop me off at another new car dealership. There I told my sad story to

Bob the salesman, who promised me that I would be able to buy a car at his dealership. This dealership specialized in high risk customers, he said, and that's what I was. But if I was willing to put down $1,000 — all the money in my checking account — they would approve the loan without a co-signer. Thrilled that I was going to get a brand new car, I once again filled out the lengthy new car application and patiently waited in Bob's office to be approved.

Forty-five minutes later, Bob strode back into his office and proudly announced that I had been approved for a vehicle. Yippee! With my heart pounding wildly, I followed Bob through the crowded showroom, past the sportscars, past the luxury sedans, past the compact cars, all the way to the back of the showroom. "Here's the car!" Bob said enthusiastically. That's when I saw that he was pointing at a small stationwagon, the least sexy car in the showroom. The Little Stationwagon That No One Else Wanted. But at least it was blue, my favorite color. So without even test driving it, I signed all the paperwork and drove it out of the dealership, feeling like the happiest person on earth!

Years later when I learned how interest rates work, I would discover that the 19 percent interest rate at which my loan was financed was astronomically high. I probably hold the world record for the highest interest rate ever paid on a new car loan. Bob the salesman probably has a plaque on his office wall for selling The Little Stationwagon That No One Else Wanted at 19 percent interest. On the bright side, however, the transaction established good credit in my name, so I never again had trouble getting approved for new car purchases, credit cards or apartment leases. Because before you establish credit, you don't exist. But after you establish good credit, everyone's anxious to get you *deep* in debt.

My neighbors at the apartment complex were very impressed with my brand new car, but they weren't very impressed when Tammy and I invited them into our apartment. It was a nice, second-story apartment with two bedrooms, two bathrooms and a scenic view through a huge picture window in the living room, but we didn't have any furniture. Not even beds. We were both sleeping in sleeping bags on the carpeted floor of our empty bedrooms. Our dining table was a large box turned upside down, and we sat on smaller boxes around it. We were saving money to buy beds, which was easier for Tammy, since she owned her five-year-old sportscar, but I was making new car payments. And I needed more clothes, as I was still living out of the one suitcase Jack had let me bring on the trip. Clearly I needed a part-time job to earn extra money, but where should I apply?

Our apartment was just down the street from a two-story shopping mall, so after work one day while I was still dressed in my business suit and high heels, I went to the mall in search of a part-time job. What store would be the most fun to work in? There were plenty of women's clothing stores, and my mom had enjoyed working in those. Then suddenly, I saw it. There was a lingerie store in this mall! Now *that* would be a fun place to work! I went in, asked if they needed any help during weekday evenings and handed my resume to the store manager, a well-dressed, middle-aged lady. She hired me on the spot and said I could start working the next day.

Selling lingerie in that store was, without question, the funnest job I ever had. Every weeknight and Saturday I worked there with Vivian, a tall black woman who could sell lingerie to people who didn't even *know* they needed lingerie. And she didn't just sell one item — she would create a sexy ensemble that highlighted the woman's physical assets, camoflauged her figure flaws, and made her feel like a goddess. Those were the female customers. We also had men come in and buy sexy outfits for their wives or girlfriends. They would spend up to $200 for a matching shelf bra, garter belt, stockings, and fur-trimmed high heels, imagining that their lover would wear the outfit and make their wildest sexual fantasy come true. Then the shocked woman would return the outfit, loudly announcing that she would *never* wear anything so sleazy, and we would help her pick out something more conservative, like a white, lace-trimmed nightgown and matching robe.

Vivian and I became a great sales team. All the black customers gravitated to her, and all the white customers asked me for help. We understood that they were more comfortable being seen nearly naked by someone of their own race. Because in this lingerie store, the sales clerk went into the fitting room with the customer to ensure a proper fit. That was interesting for me, a girl who had never worn a shelf bra *or* a garter belt. But Vivian taught me everything I needed to know. In fact, she even rescued me one time when a white man in his late twenties came in and told me he was looking for a corset. I led him over to the rack of corsets and asked him what size his lady wore. "Oh, honey, it's for *me*," he said. "What size do you think would fit me?" As I stood there flabbergasted and unable to move or speak, Vivian calmly said, "A size 12 would probably fit you, but let me get you a 12 and a 14, and you can try them both on." She grabbed two corsets, hung them in the nearest fitting room, and instructed him to try one on. Then when he said he was ready, she went into the fitting room, laced him up and told him how great he looked. And he bought the $80 corset. From then on, Vivian helped all the gay customers.

One busy Saturday afternoon when all the sales girls were working, an older man came into the store wearing a cowboy hat, cowboy boots and a big belt buckle that screamed "I'm rich." He walked up to the counter and asked our manager if any of her sales girls had pretty legs and would be interested in modeling for a television commercial. To my surprise, everyone looked at me. He said his name was Roy, he owned a cattle ranch north of Houston, his hobby was photography, and he had a client that wanted a hosiery commercial. Would I meet him at the mall next Saturday morning to film it? He would buy me a new outfit to wear and pay me $200 in cash, and I could keep the new clothes. Well, I didn't have to think twice about it, because I needed money. As they say in Texas, *Yeah, buddy*!

The next Saturday morning I met Roy at the mall's entrance, and we went shopping together for my new outfit at a trendy clothing boutique and a shoe store inside the mall. I was quite certain that the salespeople in these stores thought he was my sugar daddy, but I was so excited about my modeling gig that I didn't care. Roy bought me a cute denim mini-skirt, a red and white striped top, a pair of silky pantyhose and a pair of high-heeled, spaghetti-strap shoes, which I wore out of the stores. Then we headed over to the mall's center court, where there was a grand staircase that led to the second floor. That would be an ideal TV commercial, Roy said, me walking up and down the staircase. When we arrived at the center court, we were shocked to see that the whole area had been decorated for a fashion show. Red carpet lined the staircase and balloons and flowers were everywhere. And there was a crowd of people standing around, waiting for the fashion show to begin. Feeling like a supermodel, I walked as gracefully as I could up and down the staircase, smiling at the crowd and occasionally pausing to smile directly into Roy's video camera. He filmed me for 15 minutes, but it seemed like an hour because I was so nervous. Wouldn't the fashion show people be showing up any time now and kicking us off their set? But we got our video footage and scurried away before they arrived. And as we were leaving the mall we both laughed and laughed, because the people in the crowd had watched us in awe thinking I was a professional model and he was a professional photographer! Then Roy gave me $200 in cash, and we waved goodbye. That was my 15-minute modeling career.

"You are *so* lucky!" Tammy said when I told her about the photo shoot. But I thought *she* was the lucky one, because every night when I got home from working two jobs, she was sitting around the apartment relaxing and chatting with our neighbors. I, on the other hand, had no social life. All I did was work six days a week and then do laundry and grocery shopping on Sunday. My moonlighting earnings had allowed me to buy the bare necessities — a bed, a chair, an ironing board, a vacuum cleaner and some clothes — but as much as I liked working in the lingerie store, I had to quit. The ladies were all sorry to see me go, especially Vivian. She made me promise to always carry in my purse at all times the little black bottle of mace she had given me. And since I was living in the big city now, I did.

Most of our neighbors at the apartment complex were single adults, and they kept telling us about all the great nightclubs in Houston. I had just turned 21 and Tammy was 23, so we were both old enough to drink. And now that I no longer had to work on Friday and Saturday nights at the lingerie store, I had the time and energy to go out. Only trouble was, Tammy and I had completely different tastes in music. She was a die-hard country music fan who thought the world's greatest musical artist was singer-songwriter Willie Nelson. I was a dedicated rock and roll fan who thought the world's greatest artist was singer-songwriter Bob Seger. Tammy wanted to go to the Desperado, a country music dance club, and I wanted to go to Rockers, a rock and roll dance club. Since it wouldn't be safe for either one of us to walk into a nightclub alone, we decided to go to both clubs, the Desperado on Friday night and Rockers on Saturday night.

One hundred smiling cowboys watched us walk into the Desperado. They looked like drovers who had just finished a cattle drive, except they weren't dirty. It was a two-story nightclub with a circular balcony on the second floor, so everyone had a perfect view of the round wooden dance floor on the ground level. The dance floor was the stage, lit from above by flashing colored lights. As soon as we bought our drinks at the bar, walked over next to the dance floor, and set our drinks down on the wooden ledge, a tall man asked Tammy to dance. All eyes were on Tammy as they did the Texas two-step around the dance floor. In her cowboy hat, Western-style shirt, Wrangler blue jeans and cowboy boots, she looked like a real Texas cowgirl. Her brown, straight, waist-length hair twirled as she moved. And she knew how to do all the different types of country dancing. After each dance, she came back to where I was standing, and then another cowboy would ask her to dance. At the Desperado, Tammy was the dancing queen.

A few guys asked me to dance, but I told them I didn't know how to two-step. They probably thought I was brushing them off, but I really couldn't two-step. Tammy had tried to teach me how before we left the apartment. Stepping twice in one direction and then only once in the other direction just didn't come easily to me. So I stood there and watched everyone else dance. Finally one brave tall cowboy said he would teach me to two-step. I let him lead me out onto the dance floor, and as soon as he started two-stepping, I stepped on one of his snazzy cowboy boots. Oops. Then I did it again. Darn. This two-stepping was hard. Just when I thought he was going to give up on me and walk me back to my post, he lifted me up in the air, as though he were dancing with a doll. Now he could dance, because my legs were dangling above his boots. And dance he did. As we spun around, I looked around. People were pointing at us and laughing. That's when I knew that from then on, if a guy asked me to dance during a Texas two-step, I should just say no.

Later that night when the disc jockey played the "Cotton Eyed Joe" song and everyone linked arms and started line dancing, Tammy literally dragged me back on stage. "Just do what we do," she said, so I tried to emulate their movements. And I started catching on. Because the Cotton Eyed Joe dance is basically stepping forward and backward, kicking your feet in the air, and yelling, "bullshit," at regular intervals in the song. I could do that. By the end of the song I was feeling pretty confident about my dancing, so I courageously yelled, "bullshit," when I thought it was time. Nope. My lone yell echoed across the dance floor. All eyes stared at me, then everyone laughed, and I heard a man's voice say, "Welcome to Texas, darlin."

But I found *my* dancing heaven the very next night when we went to Rockers. It was a small nightclub, where about 50 people were standing around watching a rock band blast out popular radio hits such as Bob Seger's "Rock and Roll Never Forgets." As soon as we got our drinks and found a place to stand near the dance floor, a guy with long brown hair asked me to dance, and we assumed center stage on the dance floor. Here I was the dancing queen, because I knew how to rock and roll. In fact, back home I had dated a guy in a rock band who looked like Bob Seger, and my girlfriends and I used to go to different clubs and watch his band play almost every weekend. So I fit right into the rock club scene, with my shoulder-length, curly blond hair, red and white striped top, denim mini-skirt and high heels (garnered from my 15-minute modeling career). I danced with every guy that asked me to dance to every song the band played, and then when the band took a break, the disc jockey played *really* good dance songs, so I danced to those, too. Meanwhile, Tammy stood and watched, chatting with a guy who was trying to talk her into dancing. But she didn't know how to rock and roll. Go figure. From then on whenever we wanted to go out dancing, we went to both nightclubs — the Desperado on Friday night and Rockers on Saturday night, or vice versa — so Tammy and I could take turns being the dancing queen. Then after the bar closed, we went to Burger King. Because all that dancing worked up an appetite.

I actually got to meet Bob Seger while I was living in Houston. He came to perform a sold-out concert at The Summit, an acoustically perfect concert hall, and my friend Shelly drove 1,300 miles, all the way from Kalamazoo to Houston, just to go to the Friday night concert with me. Because like me, Shelly was a serious Bob Seger fan. The concert was awesome — Bob sang all of our favorite songs. After the concert, I told Shelly that my boss at Pumpmore Petroleum had heard that Bob Seger was going to be staying at the luxury hotel near our office building. "Let's go!" she said, so we jumped into my little stationwagon, and I drove over to the hotel. We walked into the elegant hotel lobby, looked around, and then stood there, trying to blend in, watching people arrive and glancing down at our watches as if we were there to meet someone. And what do you know, in walked Bob Seger, dressed in faded blue jeans, a black t-shirt and a black blazer.

He walked right up to where Shelly and I were standing. "Hello, my name is Shelly, I'm from Kalamazoo, Michigan, and I'm one of your biggest fans," I heard Shelly say in a polite, sophisticated tone of voice. Bob reached out to shake hands with her, and she shook his hand. Then he looked at me. Now I was so excited to be standing face to face with my rock and roll idol that I couldn't say a word. Bob was waiting for me to introduce myself, and I just smiled a huge, silly smile and froze. "This is my friend, Nancie," Shelly said. "Nice to meet you," Bob said, and held out his hand toward me. That broke the spell, and I lunged forward awkwardly to shake his hand. Then he smiled and walked past us into the hotel.

I couldn't believe how badly I had blown my chance encounter with Bob. Me, who was working in a public relations department at the time. I was more eloquent at age six when I met Michael Landon, Little Joe Cartright on "Bonanza," at a small town rodeo. I politely asked him, "Mr. Landon, Would it be alright if I gave you a kiss?" He smiled and said yes, and I kissed him on the cheek. So in Houston, I missed my chance to kiss Bob Seger or at least give him my phone number. Who knew? If I hadn't acted so stupid, I might have ended up being his next young wife.

The trouble with living in the big city is as soon as you develop a close, rewarding friendship, your single friend meets the man of her dreams and gets married and moves away. That happened time and time again. Then it happened to me. I met the man I would marry, Dale, in the hallway at

Pumpmore Petroleum. He was a petroleum engineer who had just been transferred to Houston from Midland, Texas. I was working at my desk and suddenly an attractive, dark-haired, bearded man was standing in front of the elevators, staring at me. Feeling confident because I was having a good hair day, I said hello. "Well, hello," Dale said, as if he had just discovered a new oilfield. A few days later he asked me out to lunch, and we began dating each other exclusively. And like my friends and their husbands, Dale and I decided to move away from Houston. But we still miss the Tex-Mex food.

# Chapter 7

# Smart, Very Smart

Believe it or not, the top 10 list of the world's smartest animals includes the North American gray squirrel, the cute, bushy-tailed critter that scurries up and down trees in many people's backyards. According to *USA Today*, the list is as follows:

1. Apes & Monkeys
2. Dolphins & Whales
3. Dogs
4. Cats
5. Crows
6. Ravens
7. Parrots
8. Pigs
9. Squirrels
10. Squid and Octopus

Squirrels *are* smart, very smart. A woman in the United Kingdom raised an orphan squirrel, thereby turning her house into a giant squirrel cage. Theda Kane named her pet squirrel Oz. Squirrels will investigate anything, she reported. "I had to give up wearing stud earrings, as Oz kept taking them out of my earlobes and putting them in his mouth," Kane told *USA Today*. "He also methodically removed all the buttons from my favorite cardigan and persistently stole my cigarette lighter."

A friend of mine, Mike, didn't know how smart squirrels are, because he grew up in a rural area of Michigan that didn't have any squirrels. After his children grew up and left home, he moved into a house in the city of Kalamazoo and built a three-foot-tall wooden bird feeder so his wife could enjoy watching birds feast in their backyard. As soon as he filled the feeder with bird food, along came a gray squirrel, who saw this new backyard addition as people see a buffet on a cruise ship. Free food! Yeah, buddy! Then more squirrels came to enjoy the free buffet. It was a squirrel party!

Mike was so frustrated with these furry raiders that he tried to trap them in mousetraps. He nailed 10 mousetraps to the bird feeder's wooden post, covering all four sides of the post, so the squirrels would have to climb over the mousetraps as they scaled the post. Then he waited for the first squirrel to come along. Within the hour, a gray squirrel came to investigate the upgraded bird feeder. Noticing that something was different, the squirrel sniffed and studied the post. Hmm. Then one at a time, it sprang all 10 mousetraps by barely touching each trap with its front paw. Now that the post was once again safe for squirrels, it happily ran up the post and enjoyed a nice meal.

Mike re-set the mousetraps every day for a week, but every day the same scenario occurred. The first squirrel that came along sprung all 10 traps before advancing up the post. Mike's wife, Sue, said it was one of the funniest things she had ever seen.

The tree squirrel is one of the few wild animals that has adapted to humans and learned to coexist with man. Back in ancient Greece, Aristotle named squirrels "skiouros" which means "he who sits in the shadow of his tail." Centuries later the French called them "esquirels" and the modern "squirrel" evolved from that. Like humans, squirrels have opposable thumbs. And they play, which experts say is a sign of intelligence.

Ever wonder how fast a squirrel can run? An Illinois state police officer clocked a gray squirrel with his radar gun doing 20 miles per hour as it ran across the highway. I guess that's how they can run away from dogs so easily. A squirrel will wait until a dog is only three feet away and then outrun the dog to a tree, climb up the tree and then look down, as if it were laughing at the dog. Some people call that playing. I call it taunting, and in football, that would get you a 15-yard penalty.

Squirrels are loners in nature. Adult squirrels normally live alone in a nest built into a hollow tree or between tree branches. In severely cold weather, an adult squirrel will share its nest with other squirrels to conserve body heat. But once the temperature warms up, the guests will no longer be welcome.

When you see two squirrels chasing each other at high speeds in trees and performing amazing acrobatic feats, that's their mating dance. Female squirrels choose the strongest male as a mating partner, but they are unlikely to breed with the same male again. That's nature's way of reducing inbreeding, and it explains why there are 365 different species of squirrels. Baby squirrels are called juveniles, and they are born blind, without teeth or hair. The mother squirrel raises her babies alone, and if her nest becomes infested with parasites, she will build a new nest elsewhere and move the babies one at a time, carrying them in her mouth. My husband and I saw this occur in our neighbor's front yard. Three times in a row, the mother squirrel scurried up their maple tree, then came down the tree holding a brown, egg-shaped baby squirrel gently between her razor-sharp teeth in her slightly opened mouth and ran in the same pattern toward another tree in our neighbor's backyard. So if you see that in your backyard, rest assured that the mother squirrel is *not* eating her young. She just found a better apartment.

I didn't realize how smart squirrels are until I happened to see a TV show on the Travel Channel called, "The Top 10 Places to See the World's Smartest Animals." Thinking this was going to be an *actual* top 10 list of the world's smartest animals, not a list of the top 10 tourist destinations where smart animals can be seen, my husband and I watched the show as they counted down. Number 10, squid and octopus. Number 9, squirrels. Number eight, pigs. Dale and I looked down at our calico cat, Peaches, and wondered how smart cats are. "Surely cats must be in the top 10," I said, and Dale agreed. So we sat there and watched this hour-long show, waiting for cats to be profiled. Number four, elephants. When they got down to number two, dolphins, I started worrying. "Cats *can't* be the world's smartest animal," I said. "That must be monkeys." And I was right. When the show ended, Dale and I looked down at Peaches with disappointment and disgust. "You're not as smart as a *squirrel?*" I said to Peaches. Peaches looked up at me and blinked. But later that day, I researched the topic online and found the actual top 10 list of the world's smartest animals, which lists cats at number four. What a relief.

# Chapter 8

# Practical or Too Frugal?

A friend of mine works in a large government office building that's supervised by a man who *never* gets haircuts. Once a year he shaves his head, and the rest of the year, he lets his brown hair grow long. So for the first two months of every year, he resembles a giant hedgehog. This same supervisor buys a new suit only once a year and wears it to work every day. He tells people he does these things in the name of frugality, so he never has to pay for a haircut and saves hundreds of dollars on clothing. I say that's being *too* frugal.

Don't get me wrong, I think frugality is a good thing. That's how my Dutch grandparents raised 10 children during the Great Depression. But there are different degrees of frugality. There's practical, and there's too frugal.

Practical is stocking up on freshly-harvested apples every fall so you'll have fresh apples all winter. Grandma and Grandpa VanderStel did this every year so their kids would never go hungry during the cold winter months when produce was much more expensive. They would buy apples by the bushel from a farmer and organize the 10 children into an assembly line. The kids washed the apples thoroughly, then dried each apple, wrapped it in a piece of newspaper, and packed it into the bushel baskets. Then Grandpa carried the baskets downstairs and stored them in the basement. Because properly preserved apples have a shelf life of six months. *That's* smart.

Too frugal is wrapping up and presenting to someone as a gift an item you fished out of a trash dumpster. I know a woman who does this. Janet dumpster dives on a regular basis, cleans the items as well as she can, and then stores them in her garage. Whenever someone she knows has a birthday, she goes "shopping" for a birthday present in her garage. Her friends know they've been re-gifted because the item doesn't look new, but they have no idea it spent the night in a trash dumpster.

Janet claims that her hobby is practical because she's recycling, and you must admit that Americans today are pretty wasteful. She finds the best stuff in the trash dumpsters on the university campus at the end of each semester when college students are moving out. Today's college students throw away perfectly good things like computer equipment, tables, lamps, and college textbooks. Janet returns these textbooks to the university bookstore, where she receives up to $35 in cash for each one. Then some unsuspecting college student buys the used textbook and spends 18 weeks with his or her face in it while snacking on cheese curls. Attention all college students — if you buy used textbooks, spray them down with disinfectant. Because you don't know *where* they've been.

Practical is using a teabag twice before you throw it away. Too frugal is insisting that people use each teabag four times before throwing it away. A boss I worked for at an insurance agency made me and all the other office workers do this. Let me warn ya, by the time a teabag has been used twice, it's spent. Those third and fourth of cups of "tea" taste like hot water. And c'mon, teabags aren't that expensive.

Practical is using an uncooked egg white as a facial mask. You spread it on your face, wait until it hardens, and then wash it off with warm water. Too frugal is using cat litter to make a facial mask. First, you grind clean cat litter in your blender. Then you mix it with water until it becomes clay and spread it on your face. I read this "tightwad tip" online and was horrified, because it means someone actually did this. Who is *that* desperate to tighten their pores? And who would want to use a blender to mix food and beverages after it had been used to grind cat litter?

Reusing plastic grocery bags for trash or to transport wet bathing suits and towels is practical. Reusing vacuum cleaner bags is too frugal. Can you imagine the mess that emptying a vacuum cleaner bag would make? You'd be choking on airborne dirt and dust particles for hours. And cutting old plastic gloves into homemade rubber bands? *That* would be tedious. Another frugal tip suggested using old newspapers for cleaning glass and windows. Wouldn't that smear newsprint ink on all your windows, thereby causing them to look dingy and old? I thought the whole point of cleaning windows is to make them look cleaner.

Some people think re-gifting is practical, but others think it's being too frugal. In my mind, re-gifting Christmas presents is fine as long as it's a new item that has never been used and you know the person will like it. Scented candles, for example. I can't burn scented candles because of my allergies, but every once in a while, some well-meaning person gives me a beautiful new scented candle in a fancy jar. Why shouldn't I save it in my hallway closet — the final resting place for seemingly everything in the universe — and re-gift it to someone who loves scented candles? It seems like a total waste to just throw it away, and I'd feel silly donating a candle to charity. I don't think anyone's in desperate need of a scented candle.

Probably, everyone has a hallway closet or storage area where they keep gifts they've never used, fun things like singing and dancing Santas, decorative birdhouses and oriental backscratchers, and the reason re-gifting hasn't gained wide acceptance yet is no one has set down any re-gifting rules. Please allow me:

1.  The item cannot have been procured by dumpster diving. Sorry, Janet.

2.  The item must look clean and new. Singing and dancing Santas, for example, must be dust-free, in good working order and still in the box they came in. (Note: Always save the boxes!)

3.  The gift must be something the recipient would like to receive and it must be appropriate. Do not re-gift a mustache and beard trimmer to your aunt. Do not re-gift a "Will Cook For Sex" barbeque apron to your father-in-law. And do not re-gift a coffee mug that says, "I Thought I Wanted a Career, Turns Out I Just Wanted the Paychecks" to your boss.

I think everyone has different standards for whether money-saving techniques are practical or too frugal, because frugality is a matter of personal taste. For example, a retired business owner I know could easily afford to shop at the most expensive full-service grocery store in town, yet he buys generic food from one of those pay-with-cash-only, bag-your-own-groceries bargain stores. I guess he craves the joy of bargain shopping more than he does the taste of gourmet foods. But at least he gets haircuts.

# Chapter 9

# Radio Daze

Have you ever wondered what it would be like to have a glamorous broadcasting job in television or radio? I did more than wonder about it. I took a series of broadcasting courses at the Columbia School of Broadcasting's Houston campus and earned a broadcasting degree. With my FCC broadcasting license in hand, I was ready to become the next Dan Rather. He was discovered while reporting on a hurricane in Galveston, Texas in 1961. Surely I would be discovered, too! With irrational exuberance, I left a high-paying job as an executive secretary at Pumpmore Petroleum in Houston to accept a low-paying job as a radio news reporter in a tiny town in southern Texas. It was about 100 miles from Houston, in the middle of nowhere. There were only two radio stations, a syndicated radio station that played top 40 hits, and the station I worked for, a country western radio station I'll call KSUX. We were the "WKRP in Cincinnati" of the Texas airwaves, the lovable losers.

When I accepted this glamorous radio job, I didn't realize how dangerous rural Texas was. My first day on the job, I almost died. After the station manager showed me my desk and introduced me to the station's other employees, I decided to take a picture of the small building we worked in so I could mail the photo with a letter to my parents in Michigan. It was summertime, so I was wearing open-toed, high-heeled shoes. I grabbed my camera and walked outside. The radio station was built in the center of a big field of ragged-looking grass and weeds, and a circular driveway led up to the building. Standing in the driveway in front of the building, I thought the picture would be more impressive from a distance because it would include the tower antenna, so I stepped back into the field without looking where I was stepping. There, that looked good through the viewfinder. I snapped a photo and immediately felt intense pain all over my left foot. Looking down, I noticed that my left foot was covered with black ants. Irritated, I brushed them off my foot and shoe and walked back into the radio station. "Wow, my foot *really* hurts!" I told Dave, the afternoon disc jockey. He looked down at my foot, which was swelling up like a balloon. "You got stung by Texas *fire ants*!" he said. "Didn't y'all *know* there's fire ants all over that field?"

The station manager, the bookkeeper, the receptionist and Dave were now standing in front of me, staring at me. "You don't look so good," they said. "Are you allergic to fire ants?" I told them I didn't know whether I was or not, so they decided that someone should drive me to the hospital, and Dave volunteered. "The hospital? For ant bites?" I asked. "Fire ants are *poisonous*," they said. *Oh*, I didn't know that. The town's tiny hospital wasn't far away, but that ride seemed like an eternity. My foot felt like it was on fire. I guess that's why they call them *fire* ants. My fingers were swelling up. Then Dave looked over at me and said my eyelids were swelling up, too. "Don't look in the mirror," he said.

When we arrived at the hospital, a concerned nurse rushed me into the emergency room and instructed me to lie down on the metal examination table. "We need to take off all of your clothes except for your bra and panties," she said, pulling off my blouse and skirt. A doctor rushed in and injected some kind of antidote into my left arm. Now my left arm hurt, too. Then my body reacted to the antidote and my arms and legs started shaking uncontrollably. "Am I going to die?" I asked the nurse, because I was really scared. "I don't *think* so," she replied thoughtfully. A firm "no" would have been more comforting.

As I laid there shaking on the cold metal table, strange thoughts went through my mind. "What if I *am* dying? I'm only 25 years old! And *why* did this have to happen on a day when I had to wear black underwear because all my white underwear was in my dirty clothes pile? Here I am, dying in a strange town wearing only a black bra and black panties." I could see the headline the local newspaper would run for the story: "Slutty stranger dies in local emergency room — 'If only someone had warned her about fire ants,' doctor laments."

An hour later after my heartrate and blood pressure had stabilized, the doctor said I could leave but told me to go home and spend the rest of the day in bed. Dave drove me back to the radio station, where my new boss and co-workers were happy to see that I was still alive, and I drove to my new apartment and collapsed from exhaustion.

I wasn't *on* a news team at KSUX, I *was* the news team. Small market radio stations only have one news person, and that person does all the news gathering and reporting. Every morning I started my day by going to the sheriff's department to pick up crime reports for the previous day. That was weird for me, a person who had never rubbed elbows with uniformed men that carry loaded guns. But the men were very nice and polite — they didn't make fun of my big-city hair and fashions or my Midwestern accent — and sometimes the crime reports contained actual news, not just another stolen bicycle. Then I drove to the radio station and started making phone calls and writing news reports.

I was responsible for five daily news reports, local news at 7 a.m. and 8 a.m., regional news at 12 noon, and local news at 5 p.m. and 6 p.m. And not just on weekdays, six days a week! So I had to record some of my news reports, because I didn't want to live inside the radio station. And my listeners couldn't tell the difference between Nancie's voice live or Nancie's voice on tape. One day while I was driving down main street, I pulled up next to another car at a traffic light and looked over and saw my upstairs neighbor. He recognized me and rolled down his car window, and we were both listening to my "live" news report on KSUX. "Ah hah!" he said, and we both laughed. Now he knew my secret.

My upstairs neighbor and most of the men in the town worked at a nuclear power plant that was 20 miles away, and one of my adventures during my first week in town was visiting this scary place. The plant manager wanted to give me a personal tour, the station manager said, and for safety reasons, I should wear sensible shoes, not high heels. So all by myself, I drove out to the plant. It was huge and grey and very impressive. The central control room had 10 times more buttons and switches than the cockpit of a jet airplane. "Don't touch anything," the plant manager instructed me. Are you *kidding*? I thought. I'm afraid to breathe, much less touch anything.

The plant manager described how each of the plant's comprehensive back-up safety systems worked and said that no radiation had ever leaked out at this plant. That made me feel better. Then just when I was starting to feel safe, he suggested that we get into a golf cart and tour the grounds. He drove this golf cart over to the plant's cooling pond and parked right next to the pond. As he was describing the vital role a cooling pond plays in the nuclear power generation process, a large alligator crawled out of the pond six feet away from us and looked at us. It took all of my willpower to *not* scream. "What's that alligator doing in the cooling pond?" I asked. "Oh, they like it, so they hang around all the time," the plant manager replied calmly. I still don't know *why* that alligator didn't crawl over to the open golf cart and take a nice big bite out of my leg, but I assume it was because he wasn't hungry. But from that day on, I wondered about those alligators. Could they somehow be affected by the plant's radiation? Were they creating giant supergators that would eat their way into town and ambush me as I walked out of my ground-floor apartment? I actually had a nightmare about that.

My first local election coverage was interesting. Not entirely factual, but entertaining. I had only been on the job for a week and had never covered an election before, but Paul, the program director, came back to the radio station after his dinner break to help me with the 7 o'clock broadcast. Fifteen minutes before I was to go on the air, Paul rushed into the recording booth where I was sitting and handed me a 10-page computer spreadsheet that listed all the candidates and the winner of each race. As I read them aloud to practice these unfamiliar names, he told me whether I was pronouncing them correctly. Then right before 7 o'clock, Paul went into the control booth where Dave was ending his afternoon show. I could see them through the window between the recording booth and the control room, and when Dave gave me the cue, I started reading the list.

Now I probably would have been okay if I had stuck to reading the basic information on the computer spreadsheet, but *no*, I wanted to impress my new audience. I read for 20 minutes straight, enhancing the report with commentary such as, "In the race for city mayor, Johnny Walker beat Vern Farnsworth by a landslide, winning 78 percent of the votes." When I finished reading the results of every race in the tri-county area, the disc jockey who produced the evening show took over the microphone in the control room, and I breathed a huge sigh of relief. Then Paul and Dave came into the recording booth laughing hysterically, and I noticed they were both drinking cans of beer. "Y'all know the two guys with the same last name that y'all said were father and son?" Paul asked me. "They're *not* father and son. One of them's white and the other one's black!" I was horrified, but they told me not to be upset and that our listeners would probably think it was funny because they knew I was new in town. Paul opened a can of beer and handed it to me. "Welcome to small market radio," he said, and the three of us raised our beer cans in a toast to my first election coverage as a radio news reporter.

Being an on-air radio personality *was* fun, especially when we did live remote broadcasts. We had a super saleswoman, Sonya, who in addition to selling radio advertising somehow convinced local business owners to pay KSUX hundreds of dollars for the privilege of having us come to their business on a Saturday and stand around and chat live on the radio between songs about how great their products were and how everyone should drop everything they were doing and rush over to where we were. Or if Sonya didn't sell a live remote broadcast and there was a fair or a festival in the area, we would all go to the event to promote our radio station. Paul, Dave, Sonya and I would ride to these events in our radio station's official vehicle. It was an old yellow motor home with a tacky magnetic yellow and brown sign on each side that read, "KSUX Country Camper."

People actually *did* listen to us, I learned during these remote broadcasts. They would see us standing around the Country Camper wearing our KSUX t-shirts and point at us and get all excited and come over to say hello and shake our hands. For some reason when people met me for the first time, they felt compelled to give me an on-the-spot performance review. "*You're* Nancie Boss?" they would say. "I *like* you," as if that surprised even them. In return for this celebrity treatment, we gave them ugly yellow and brown KSUX bumper stickers. Then just when we were feeling really good about ourselves and our radio station, the other radio station's crew would arrive in their brand new black van with the custom paint job and the state-of-the-art stereo that blasted out top 40 hits. Which was kind of like having someone drive up in a new sportscar while you're showing off your new little stationwagon — suddenly, you don't feel nearly as cool. But we had programming they didn't have, my local and regional news reports. Their station only broadcast national news reports. Hah! A competitive edge. And because everyone tuned into KSUX to hear my news reports, I was a big star. Well, as big a star as one can be in small market radio.

One day the station manager asked me to start selling radio ads. Have you ever tried to sell something that's intangible? Selling a radio ad is not like selling a newspaper ad that the business owner can hold in their hand and post on their bulletin board. It's like selling an invisible product. They pay the money for it, hear it on the radio, and then it's just a memory. Trying to sell radio ads gave me new respect for Sonya. No wonder she was so friendly. She *had* to make people like her. I did sell a few radio ads to local business owners that knew me and wanted to sponsor my news reports, and I got to write the copy for them and produce them. Because in small market radio, you get to do it all.

For instance, when Dave went on a one-week vacation, I was asked to do part of his afternoon show. It is important to note here that Dave was an experienced disc jockey who knew everything about country music. Country *and* western. Conversely, all I knew about country music was the songs I had heard at the Desperado country dancing nightclub in Houston. And even though I had studied radio production at the Columbia School of Broadcasting, I had never actually sat in a real control room and spun records. But for one week, I would be a KSUX disc jockey every day from 12 noon to 2 p.m.

"It's *easy*," Paul said to me, as he showed me the record library. "Just pick out a bunch of records and play them, and then after the show, re-file them in the library." Okay. I looked through the library and found an album that contained Alabama's greatest hits. There were four songs that I recognized! Yeah, buddy! I pulled a few more greatest hits albums by well-known country artists such as George Strait and Dolly Parton and then headed into the control room. Paul showed me how to cue up a song on one of the two record players and pointed out the buttons that switched my microphone on and off. Then he left the radio station, leaving me all alone in the control room on my first day as a substitute disc jockey. I haven't asked a lawyer, but I think that's employee abandonment.

With my heart pounding wildly, I waited for the 12:00 national news broadcast to end and then gave my regular regional news report. "And I'll be staying with you today and every day this week until 2 o'clock, because I'm filling in for Dave while he's on vacation," I said to the audience. Then I played an Alabama song. So far, so good. Only one hour and fifty minutes to go. While one song was playing, I cued up another song on another album on the other record player. I also had to remember to play the commercials that were scheduled to air during each hour. I had to answer the phone whenever a listener called in with a request. And there could be no silence, or as they say in the radio biz, dead air.

Disc jockeys have to carefully schedule all songs, commercials and public service announcements so the last one ends precisely two seconds before the top of the hour, which leaves them just enough time to announce the station's call letters — a legal FCC requirement — and then say, "And now, the national news." That's called back-timing, and for someone like me who never liked math and depended on a calculator just to balance my checkbook, it seemed impossible. But I did it by playing the same songs every day, songs I knew were exactly three minutes long. In fact, I'm surprised none of my listeners called in and pleaded, "*Please*! No more Alabama!" But they didn't, which proves that country music fans *never* get sick of hearing Alabama songs. Plus, I also played songs that were in the top 20 on Billboard's country music chart, such as Garth Brooks' classic hit, "I Got Friends in Low Places." Everyone *loved* that song.

When the weather was nice on Sundays, my only day off, I went to the beach. It was only a 20-minute drive, and it was a very secluded beach on the Gulf of Mexico. Because I didn't know anyone else in town very well and I didn't particularly want any of my co-workers to see me nearly naked, I went alone. There was a sign warning people to swim at their own risk and there were two portable bathrooms, one for women and one for men, but that was it. People drove their cars and trucks onto the beach and cruised as far as they wanted down the coast, then picked a spot and unloaded their folding chairs and coolers. Everyone had their own 300-yard stretch of beach that was about 200 yards wide between the sand dunes and the water's edge. I sat on mine all alone, and the people who cruised by me smiled and waved, but I couldn't help but wonder if they thought I had no friends because I was there alone. I should have held up a hand-made sign that read: All My Friends Live in Houston. Nonetheless, basking on that sandy beach on Sundays and listening to the ocean gently lapping the shoreline helped me maintain my tan and my sanity. Because the radio business is a crazy business.

One morning when I went to the sheriff's department to pick up the crime reports from the day before, the sheriff gave me a memo about a free ladies handgun safety course that was being offered to all women in the county. "Y'all should take that," Sheriff Bookum advised me, noting that without a gun, if I ever had car trouble while driving 30 miles to cover the Monday night city council meeting in the nearest town, I would be a sitting duck for the first criminal that came along. *Gee*, what a pleasant thought. The former KSUX news reporter had been a man, he said, so no one had worried about him. But the sheriff seemed genuinely concerned about *my* safety, so I agreed to promote the free ladies handgun safety course on the radio, take the course, and buy a used revolver from the sheriff for $50.

Nineteen other women signed up for the course, and on the designated Saturday morning, we all met at the sheriff's department and followed him in our cars to an open field where targets were set up about 50 feet away. After Sheriff Bookum showed us how to handle a gun safely and how to load bullets into it, we loaded our guns and aimed at the targets. Whoa! Even a small revolver makes a loud noise and jolts your body backward when it's fired. We kept practicing. When everyone's chambers were empty, the sheriff announced that it was time to "cease fire and reload," and while we were reloading, he walked out to the targets to see how well we had done. I had shot the center of the target, my first bull's eye, he announced loudly, and all the women cheered. "Ready, aim, fire!" he said. We resumed shooting until our chambers were empty again. "*Hey*, this is *fun*!" one woman said. "Now I'm *ready* for the next rattlesnake that comes into my yard!" "Rattlesnakes?" I asked. "Yes, they're everywhere," she replied. "Didn't y'all know? The sand dunes at the beach are infested with them." From that point on, I carried my gun in my car whenever I drove anywhere, especially the beach.

We never went hungry at KSUX, because the station negotiated barter agreements with local business owners that served food. Every morning the receptionist stopped at the local donut shop and picked up free donuts for us. Every Monday at lunchtime we ate free pizza. And every Friday at lunchtime we ate free beef barbeque sandwiches. In return for the free food, the businesses received free radio advertising. The Monday and Friday lunches were informal staff meetings where we would all sit around the conference table in the station manager's office and chat while happily wolfing down the free food. Looking back on it, the station manager probably decided to give us free lunches on Mondays and Fridays to discourage people from calling in sick on the days most employees call in sick. And it worked — no one ever called in sick on Monday or Friday.

It was during one of these staff meetings that I reminded my co-workers that I knew how to write press releases and newsletters. "Go for it!" they said. First, I sent out a press release on KSUX letterhead. Then I created the first KSUX newsletter. It wasn't fancy, just an 8 1/2-by-11-inch, back-and-front, one-page newsletter typed on my manual typewriter and copied onto colored paper, but the station manager thought it was fantastic. She told the receptionist to mail it to everyone in town, and we got several phone calls from people who said they really liked it. The station manager was so impressed that she promoted me from news reporter to news director! The promotion didn't come with a raise in salary, but I got a new title, printed business cards and an office, a big office between the recording studio and the bookkeeper's office. I was so happy that I bought a "Magnum P.I." poster of Tom Selleck's smiling face and put it up on the back of my office door so I could see it whenever the door was closed. Sometimes the bookkeeper, a shy, middle-aged black woman who had a great sense of humor, would come into my office just to look at it and sigh. The men had a sexy poster of Tanya Tucker on the wall of the control room that they drooled over, we rationalized. Now we women had a hunky poster in my office. You can get away with things like that in a small market radio station. It's a fun place.

Shortly after my promotion, Texas Senator Phil Gramm came to our tiny town on his whistle stop tour of southern Texas. Everyone in town donned their finest clothing and crowded into the county courthouse to hear him speak. This was my first opportunity to interview a big-time politician, so I was very excited. Too excited. I was so awestruck that he was really there that I couldn't think of a single question to ask him. So I just held up my little microcassette tape recorder and recorded his answers to the local newspaper reporter's questions. The next day, I sat down to write a one-minute broadcast news report which summarized the event and realized that I wanted to write much more than that. I wanted to write a 1,000-word article and have it printed in the newspaper, like Fred, the newspaper man I sat next to at city council meetings. Hmm. Maybe I should be a newspaper reporter, *not* a radio news reporter.

As if she sensed what I was thinking, the station manager called me into her office on my 89th day of employment and did her impression of Donald Trump. "You're fired," she said, and I knew she was serious because she had a witness sitting there watching us. Now I shouldn't have taken this firing personally, but I did, because I didn't understand that people who work in small market radio stations in tiny towns that have only one traffic light are *always* getting fired. Television talk show host Sally Jesse Raphael and her husband worked in small market radio for years, and whenever they got fired because the radio station was sold to a new owner or changed formats, they packed everything they owned, piled their young children in their car, and announced that they were going on vacation. What they really were doing was driving from town to town looking for a radio station where both could get a job, but they didn't want their kids to freak out.

That Sunday as I was packing boxes in my apartment, Paul the program director called me and reported the rest of the story. My firing had been the first in a massive layoff that had eliminated four of the radio station's 10 employees. Negotiating too many barter agreements for free advertising had caused a cash flow problem, and there wasn't enough income to pay all 10 of our salaries. So the station manager had fired me, Sonya the saleswoman, the receptionist, and the janitor. "I've already found another job and another apartment in Houston, and I'm moving back there tomorrow," I reported to Paul on the phone. "But *thanks* for letting me know that I wasn't the only one they let go."

The next day as I drove out of town, I was no longer sad. I was happy to be going back to Houston, where all my friends lived. I was excited about starting a job that paid a much higher salary. And I was looking forward to once again living in the big city, where there were no fire ants, alligators or rattlesnakes. But during the long drive back to Houston, I was still reeling from the other shocking news Paul had told me. It seems that the whole time I was working at KSUX, Sonya the saleswoman was having a secret affair with Paul *and* Dave *and* some guy who owned a shop in town. After Sonya left, the shop owner drove out to the radio station and demanded to know where she was. "I'm in love with her," he said. "I've been seeing her for the past three months." Shortly after he left, Paul confessed to Dave that he also had been having an affair with Sonya, and a stunned Dave replied, "*Me*, too!"

# Chapter 10

# Getting Creative

A few years ago I interviewed the world's greatest con artist, Frank Abagnale, whose real-life story was portrayed in the Disney movie, "Catch Me If You Can." Abagnale impersonated an airline pilot, a doctor and a security guard before being arrested and serving time in prison. Now working as a consultant with the Federal Bureau of Investigations, he came to Kalamazoo to give a group of financial services professionals a presentation on how to prevent check fraud. He had passed millions of dollars in bad checks, so he was an expert. One example in his presentation that I found particularly fascinating was the story of a desperate freelance writer in the state of New York who scanned a refund check from a utility company into his computer, changed the check amount from $250 to $250,000, printed it and cashed it at a bank but subsequently was arrested by police and ended up going to prison. After the presentation, I asked him if he just *said* the man was a freelance writer because he knew I was in the audience. "No, he *really* was a freelance writer," he replied. "And what still frustrates me is, he would have gotten *away* with it if he had also changed the name and address on the check." "I guess that's why he couldn't make any money as a freelance writer — he lacked imagination," I said. Abagnale laughed out loud and said, "You know, you're probably *right*."

Getting creative has never been a problem for me, but then I was raised by an artist, and for many years, we didn't own a television. So I had *plenty* of time on my hands. It was the hippie era, and mom and I were always making things like candles, beaded necklaces and peasant tops. Back then you were cool if your clothing expressed your individuality, so everyone sewed different embroidered trims on the bottom edge of their bell-bottom jeans. The popular saying on bumper stickers, posters and t-shirts was "Do Your Own Thing." This is the same generation, by the way, that today wears uniform-like khaki pants and light blue button-down cotton shirts that make us all look like clones.

The moment people stepped into our living room, they knew they were in a unique house, and not just because there was no television. The carpeting in our living room was green shag, which mom said represented green grass. Our couch was covered with a yellow-and-white-checkered bedspread and above it hung two yellow lamps, which represented the sun. The focal point of the room was a homemade fireplace mom had built from metal furnace pipe and lumber and bricks. Two feet out from our front picture window, mom had created a wall of green spider plants and ivy that hung like a living curtain. Between the window and the plant wall, she placed a small yet comfortable chair where one could sit and read a book or just look out the window. It was kind of like a bug's view from inside a terrarium.

Motivated by boredom, I was always creating something. When my dad gave me a cassette tape recorder, I created a radio show by recording my favorite songs as they played on my AM/FM radio and chatting like a disc jockey between songs. I wrote a book of poems and gave it to my dad on Father's Day. I created flowers using pastel-colored facial tissues and green pipe cleaners. These floral arrangements were decorative and quite practical — they never needed watering, the flowers never died, and if you ran out of facial tissue, you could always grab a flower and untwist the pipe cleaner.

Speaking of destroying a child's artwork, who was the sadist that invented that reusable colored clay that parents give to their kids? That stuff doesn't stimulate creativity in kids, it tortures kids. First, you get four different colors of clay and they tell you to have fun and create something. Then after you spend an hour or so creating a colorful clay sculpture that you're really proud of, they order you to destroy it — to rip off its arms, legs, head and facial features — and put the clay back into the plastic-lidded canisters so it will stay fresh. Up until then, I had always been allowed to *keep* all my artwork. What's the *point* of creating artwork if you have to destroy it right away?

Humor stimulates a child's creativity. A cool new babysitter introduced me to *MAD Magazine*, thereby irrevocably warping my previously normal sense of humor. From then on, I spent my weekly allowance on *MAD Magazine* and *MAD* paperback books such as Al Jaffee's *Snappy Answers to Stupid Questions*. On every page of the book was a cartoon, and above it, a stupid question, two snappy answers, and a blank line where the child could create and write in a third snappy answer. Boy, did I have fun thinking those up and writing them in. And after I was done, I didn't have to *destroy* it.

My favorite *MAD* book was a collection of satirical songs entitled, *Sing Along with MAD*, in which the humor writers for the magazine wrote new lyrics for a wide variety of classic songs, twisting "Home on the Range" into "Home is So Strange" and "Jingle Bells" into "Christmas Bills." These songs created such an impression on my young mind that I *still* remember all the words to them, and to this day, I still write funny new lyrics to new songs. I just can't help it, I have to. Martina McBride's heart-warming tribute to women everywhere, "This One's For The Girls" becomes "This One's For The Squirrels." Kenny Chesney's nostalgic anthem about youth, "We Were Mostly Young" becomes "We Were Mostly Dumb." See how fun that is?

I also can't help writing funny poems for people I know. For example, when an independent, headstrong friend of mine announced that she was getting married the first time at age 28, she told me the story of their courtship, and I wrote the following poem and surprised the bride and groom by reading it onstage at their wedding reception:

Tim the avid hunter was contented with his life,
Til one day when he realized that he needed a wife,
Now as an avid hunter, he knew where to find game,
But what about a woman who was worthy of his name?
Cindy too was looking for a wise and worthy mate,
Someone who would be good to her but wouldn't dominate,
A man who likes to talk and dance and take long hot tub soaks,
Who likes her dog and cats and fish and laughs at all her jokes,
So when they met one summer night and Tim asked her to dance,
They both were ready to begin a new summer romance,
They got to know each other and how each likes to have fun,
And when the summer was over, Tim knew she was the one,
So Tim took Cindy camping to a special place he knew,
They marveled at the scenery, and paddled a canoe,

And when the stars came out that night, he took her by
his side,
Looked deep into her eyes and asked her to become his
bride,
So now they're here today with friends and family
around,
To help them celebrate the happiness that they have
found.

Afterward, as the crowd of 150 people in the audience
cheered, I walked down off the stage and presented them
with the framed poem. That's when I noticed that Cindy
was laughing, but Tim was crying. The poem had moved
him to tears, right in front of all his tough hunting buddies.
*Gee*, I didn't mean to make the groom *cry*.

One time when I resigned from a job, I wrote a
"resignation poem" instead of a resignation letter. I had
worked at this place for some time and had made many
friends there, so a letter just seemed too formal. My boss,
Bob, was the president of the company, and I'll never forget
the look on his face when I handed the poem to him. It
began, "I really hate to say goodbye to all of you and Bob,
But soon I'll be departing to begin another job." I think he
thought I had lost my mind. Nope, I'm just a writer who
grew up reading *MAD*.

Creative is mixing together two different types of
breakfast cereal so you're eating something you've never
eaten before. That's what the chief executive officer of
the Battle Creek, Michigan-based Kellogg Company does
every morning. Yes, Carlos Gutierrez, the guy who runs
the world's largest cereal manufacturing giant, experiments
with his company's cereals to create new taste sensations in
his own kitchen every day, just like the Kellogg brothers did

in their kitchen back in the early 1900s when they invented the first breakfast cereal. I conducted a telephone interview with Gutierrez, and after he had answered all of my serious questions about the company's financial performance and marketing strategies, I asked him, "What do *you* eat for breakfast?" Then again, more than one person has told me that I'm the most inquisitive person they have ever met. Not nosy, inquisitive. That sounds better.

Creative is making up storybook characters and adventures to get your kids to learn manners. That's what my mom did when my brother and I were very young. She told us bedtime stories about Nancy If You Please, Froggie Beg Your Pardon and Bunny Oops, and there was always a moral at the end of the story about being polite. I had forgotten all about those stories until a few years ago. Sitting in my breezeway, relaxing at the end of a long day, I was staring out at our backyard flower garden and lawn ornaments. I saw the life-like, ceramic rabbit that my husband had given to me and the hand-sculpted, hand-painted green clay frog that my brother had given to me and realized that we were all there! I was Nancy If You Please, the frog was Froggie Beg Your Pardon, and the rabbit was Bunny Oops. Weird. Now whenever I look out at our backyard, my lawn ornaments remind me to always be polite.

Making creative gifts is fun, and people never forget them. When a friend of mine landed a great job as a reference librarian at a public library, I painted a pin-on, three-inch-round, campaign-style button with solid blue paint and then painted white letters which read, "Ask Me Anything." Because that was her new job, answering people's questions about everything.

When a news reporter I know won his first national news scoop award, I cut out his award-winning article, folded it so you could still read the title, date and his byline, and taped it with clear tape inside a stainless steel scoop — the kind you see in the bulk candy and nuts bins in grocery stores. So *his* news scoop article was in an *actual* scoop. I wrapped up this unique gift and surprised him with it while he was eating lunch at his desk. He loved it, and it was such a hit at the publication he works for that they initiated a news scoop incentive program for their sales staff. Now whenever one of their sales people gives a news tip to one of the reporters that results in a news scoop, the sales person receives a silver scoop. For example, one woman received an ice cream scoop and a container of gourmet ice cream. Because getting a news scoop — that is, finding out about an unknown news item and reporting it before the local daily newspaper and all other news publications do — is very hard these days. And winning a *national* news scoop award seems like a miracle!

My brother admitted to me that with each passing year he becomes more like "Red Green," the suspender-wearing Canadian do-it-yourselfer on public television who uses duct tape to fix everything, so I made a "Red Green" photo collage, framed it and gave it to Steve for Christmas. And I made it the Red Green way, not spending a dime. First, I printed out the "Red Green" home page on the PBS Web site. Next, I cut out the funniest graphics, including a full-length photo of Red Green and the intentionally silly "Man's Prayer" and pasted them up in an artistic fashion. Then I looked through the Christmas pictures I had taken the year before and found one of Steve smiling a huge smile. I cut out Steve's head and beard and pasted it over Red Green's head on the collage. It looked so funny that I couldn't stop laughing while I was making it. The collage fit perfectly into an old picture frame I found in my hallway closet. Steve loved this gift so much he took it into work and showed it to the guys, and they laughed and laughed. "They've been telling me for years that I'm turning into Red Green," he said.

However, the *most* creative gift I've ever made for someone was a squirrel reading a book. Michael Chevy Castranova, the editor of a business news publication I'd been contributing articles to for years, *Business Direct Weekly*, had just published his first book. It was a humor book that included an outrageously funny chapter about the time squirrels moved into the attic of his house. First, I saw a life-like, upright, six-inch-tall toy squirrel with brown fur and a big bushy tail in a store and bought it. Then I created a miniature version of his book, *A Perfectly Logical Explanation*, and glued it into the squirrel's front paws, so it looked like the squirrel was reading the book. The joke, of course, was that the squirrel was interested in his book because it's a squirrel-friendly book in which no squirrels are harmed. After carefully gift-wrapping the squirrel and including a nice congratulations card with it, I had it delivered to the editor. Then I worried. "He's going to think I'm *crazy* if he doesn't get the joke," I thought. But he understood the joke, thanked me, and told me it was one of the funniest things he had ever seen. And a week later, he told me the rest of the story. After opening the gift, he had displayed the book-reading squirrel prominently in his office. "Strangely, it ended up being the acid test for my staff as to whether or not they had read my new book," he reported. "All the people who came into my office and saw it and laughed — I knew they had read the book. But the people who didn't understand it and didn't laugh and asked what it meant — I knew they hadn't read the book and said, 'Ah hah!'"

Frankly, I'm worried that today people aren't as creative as they could be. Just look at our entertainment. Most new movies and TV shows are remakes of old ones. It's as if Hollywood can't come up with any new ideas. Are we doomed to watch old screenplays and sequels for the rest of our lives? Will Hollywood actually film "The Stepford Wives VII"? I remember being impressed when ABC came out with the "new" game show, "Who Wants to Be a Millionaire," and then finding out that it was based on a British TV game show. Hmm. Can't we come up with any new ideas? Has the human brain been tapped out in terms of imagination?

Nowhere is this lack of creativity more prevalent than in country music. The songwriters of today's country music copy each other shamelessly, not only stealing themes but actual phrases and melodies. It's incredible. The chorus of Terri Clark's song, "I Want To Do It All," is the same exact melody of Trisha Yearwood's hit, "Perfect Love." Why doesn't Trisha sue? I guess because she's already rich.

The advertising world is famous for recycling old ideas, but in that realm, it works. You take an old classic song, give it a new twist, and you've got an appealing jingle for a TV or radio commercial. But I always have to chuckle when a young person hears one of these jingles and thinks it's new because they've never heard the original song. Like the jingle for Fox News at 10 that talks about waiting. When I mentioned to a young girl that this particular song was stuck in my head, she replied, "You've been watching too much Fox television," thinking I had been brainwashed by the new commercial. No, I was just remembering the hit song from the '60s.

Thus, the question remains: How do we stimulate creativity in ourselves and in our children? Stephen Spielberg's mom let him smear cherry pie filling all over her kitchen cabinets and walls when he was a young lad so he could make his first horror film. He got an A on the school project, but how long did it take her to clean up that sticky mess? Because getting creative can be messy. Whenever my mom and I made wax candles in our kitchen, we spent days scraping stray drops of wax off the kitchen counters. After sewing peasant tops and beading necklaces and bracelets on the living room floor, we picked scraps of thread and beads out of the carpet for days. Then again, you can't be creative *and* clean at the same time. To be creative, you have to relax and not be afraid of making a mistake or making a mess. That's how the best art is created. But whether your kid's artwork turns out looking like garage sale merchandise or an exhibit in the Metropolitan Museum of Art, please don't destroy it. Encourage him or her to keep creating. The future of our entertainment industry may depend on it.

# Chapter 11

## But I Danced

The term "saving money" used to mean literally depositing money into a savings account. When people wanted to buy something new, they saved up for it and then bought it. Not so with today's shoppers. We see something that we want on sale and buy it today with a credit card. It's on sale, so we're *saving money*. Who wants to wait when we can have it now?

I understand this mentality, because I've always been a "now" kind of person. I also understand going to the store to buy socks on sale and returning home with a new full-length faux suede coat. "But it's *machine washable*, it was 40 percent off, and I've always wanted a coat like this!" I explained to my husband, who stared at the coat with wide eyes.

So then I had to tell the whole story. How I was just innocently walking through the women's clothing department of the store on the way to the socks aisle and saw the "40 percent off all outerwear" sign above the washable suede jackets and coats I'd had my eye on for weeks. How I tried on two dozen of them and found this one that fits perfectly, flatters my eye and hair color, and doesn't make me look fat. How trying it on while looking into the full-length mirror at the end of the aisle made me dance with joy!

At that moment, I was not an ordinary woman trying on a coat in a store. I was Faith Hill twirling onstage in concert. The spotlight beamed warmly upon me, the crowd cheered, and I radiated beauty and grace. *That's* why the other shoppers were staring at me.

However, my embarrassment that day pales in comparison with the time my brother tried to return a newly-purchased space heater to a discount superstore. His wife had bought it without opening the box and then opened the box at home and found an old, dirty, used space heater that did not look anything like the new, clean, shiny space heater pictured on the box. So she asked Steve to return it, because he was going to the store to pick up a few things anyway.

When Steve showed the clerk at the return desk his receipt and the dirty space heater inside the new box, she called for the store's assistant manager to approve the return. The assistant manager looked inside the box, glared at Steve with a disgusted look, and then in front of all the other shoppers, he said in a downright nasty tone of voice, "Leave the store *now*." Because he thought *Steve* was pulling the scam of buying a new space heater, removing it from the box, putting an old one in, and returning it for a refund. When Steve knew that someone else had done it, and his wife had been the unlucky victim.

What made this situation really ironic was the fact that Steve's son, Dan, was working in the store full-time. He had been a full-time employee there for three years while working his way through college and had just been promoted to manager of the produce department. So Steve and his family were among the store's best shoppers!

Steve was able to exchange the old space heater for a new one — after, of course, opening the box to make sure it was indeed new — with help from the store's manager. The store manager apologized to Steve, the assistant manager apologized to Steve, and they all ended up laughing about the awkward situation. Because those shoplifters can be crafty. I've interviewed store security personnel who have told me that teenagers will try on new shoes, clip the price tags off, put their old shoes in the new shoe box, return the new shoe box to the shelf, and wear the new shoes out of the store. So whenever you buy a new space heater or new shoes, always look in the box first.

But all things considered, today's shoppers have it made. Shopping is easier than ever before — you can even shop online without leaving your house — and most durable goods cost less than they have in years. That's why it's so hard to avoid the temptation of buying stuff you want now and running up credit card debt.

I learned why people have such a hard time paying off credit card debt while working at a credit union several years ago. It's the curse of compounded interest. See, with credit card debt, you are paying interest every month, and *not* just on new purchases, on the *total balance*. In layman's terms, you're not just paying interest on all the purchases you've charged, you're paying interest on all the interest charges that have accumulated on your account. So if it takes you five years to pay off the bill for that great pair of shoes you saved so much money on because they were on sale for only $29, you will end up paying $59 for them. Which, coincidentally, was the original price of the shoes before the sale.

Actually, only 40 percent of credit card holders pay their balances off every month, and many adults don't know how to manage their finances effectively. In fact, while working at that credit union, I learned that most young people who graduate from high school do not even understand how to maintain a checking account, much less how to use credit cards effectively. So I think everyone should be required to take a course during high school called "Understanding Personal Finance" that would teach us the basics. Because once you get out of school and begin working, no one will tell you how to manage your finances. There's an unwritten law of etiquette in America that forbids people from asking one another about money. While interviewing a tax accountant for an article I was writing about "A Day in the Life of an Accountant," I asked her if she ever had trouble getting people to reveal their actual financial situations. "Are you *kidding*?" she replied. "Most people are more willing to talk about their *sex* lives than they are their finances."

Back before everyone used credit cards and debit cards, debt wasn't a problem for American consumers because everyone wrote checks. That made shopping much more of a challenge — if the cashier didn't know you and if you didn't have your driver's license, social security card and voter registration in hand, he or she might refuse to cash your check. That's why my mom always shopped at the same stores where the cashiers knew her. One of them was called Fred's Trading Post, and it was there that we pulled a practical joke on my brother, Steve, when we paid for our groceries.

Fred's Trading Post was a small, charming neighborhood grocery store that looked like a log cabin. It was as if a tornado had lifted it up off a Kentucky hilltop and set it down in a Michigan suburb. Other than the decor, it was an ordinary grocery store, but my brother didn't know that. Steve was 18, and he had just come to live with mom and me so he could attend the state university in our town. I was only 10, and even though mom explained the joke to me beforehand, I didn't really understand it. But when you're 10 years old and your mom tells you to do something because it will be funny, you trust her. In fact, that's why we were able to fool Steve. Because he trusted his mom and little sister.

For several weeks, mom built suspense for the gag by telling Steve, "Oh, we *have* to take you to Fred's Trading Post one of these days." Then one sunny summer day, she announced that we were all going to go there. As we rode in the car toward the store, she told Steve that Fred's Trading Post was a *real* trading post where people traded durable goods. You couldn't even pay for your purchases with money or a check, she said. "I'm going to trade this umbrella, and Nancie's going to trade her shoelaces," she told him.

Sitting in our parked car in front of the store's big, old-fashioned wooden sign, mom instructed me to remove the shoelaces from my tennis shoes, and I did. Then she grabbed her umbrella, and we headed into the store. The three of us wandered through the aisles, filled a shopping cart half-full of groceries, and then approached the check-out lanes. Mom was holding her umbrella, and I was holding my shoelaces, as if we were ready to trade them. "What are *you* going to trade?" mom asked Steve. "I don't know," he replied. "I'm wearing loafers, so I don't have any shoelaces. All I have to trade is my belt." So he took off his leather belt. We loaded our groceries onto the check-out lane, and the cashier rung up our total sale and announced the total to Steve, who was standing in front of her. "All I have to trade is my belt," Steve said, handing her the leather belt. "Can I trade this?" he asked. The cashier looked at Steve as if he were from a distant planet. Steve turned and looked at mom, and not being able to stand it anymore, she erupted into hysterical laughter. Then we all laughed, Steve, the cashier, and the other customers who were standing around watching us in amazement. Because you can't trade an umbrella, a pair of shoelaces and a leather belt for three bags of groceries, even at Fred's Trading Post. But it sure was fun watching my brother try.

# Chapter 12

# I Could Do That

When I was in junior high school, my guidance counselor called me into his office and asked me what career I had in mind. *Gulp*. I didn't have a career in mind. I looked over at Mr. Fredericks' bookshelf, which was bulging with books about various careers and catalogs for colleges I had never heard of, as if just reading one of the titles would help me choose a career. It didn't. So Mr. Fredericks suggested that I start thinking about it.

The year was 1973, and feminists such as Gloria Steinem were leading the women's liberation movement and boldly saying that women could become anything they wanted — doctors, lawyers, engineers, accountants, scientists, police officers — professions which previously had been open only to men. Then there were all the professions that women were already in, such as teaching and nursing. For a 13-year-old girl, the possibilities were overwhelming. But I started thinking ...

Let's see. When I was four years old, I thought I could be a singer. This was based on the fact that I could sing along with Shelley Fabares' new radio hit, "Johnny Angel" and hit all the notes. My mother and I had visited a rich lady who had given me free reign over her console stereo and record collection, and I had played that song 10 times while they were having tea, so the nice lady had suggested that I take it home. (After hearing it 10 times in a row, she probably never wanted to hear it again.) But during the drive home, when I proudly announced to my mom that I could hit all the notes in my new favorite song, she frowned and replied, "Well, that's probably because Shelley Fabares has a weak voice and a limited vocal range. That's why the backup singers sing all the high notes." *Oh.* So my voice wouldn't land me a singing career.

When I was seven years old, I decided that I wanted to become a nurse when I grew up. I could wear those pretty white uniforms and follow the doctor around and help people when they needed kindness and comfort most — wouldn't that be great? My mom approved of that career aspiration, and I thought I had a winner ... until I accidentally scraped the roof of my mouth with a thin, eight-inch-long, red metal pipe that was a make-believe flute while dancing around my bedroom dressed in a white sheet, pretending I was an angel. I looked in the mirror, saw blood running down my tongue, screamed and fainted. When I woke up in the emergency room, I knew that I didn't have what it takes to be a nurse. A nurse has to be able to see blood without fainting.

When I was 11 years old, I thought I could become the fastest runner in the world. This was based on my street races with Pepsi, the brown, six-month-old, German shepherd-chow mix puppy that my brother had given to me as a surprise for my birthday. Joyfully Pepsi and I would race down the quiet street where we lived — it was a cul-de-sac with no traffic other than our neighbors, so it was safe — running as fast as we could, until I was out of breath. Every day that summer, Pepsi and I raced. Ready, set, go! At first, Pepsi would always outrun me and glance back at me gleefully as I struggled to keep up. After three weeks, we ran at the same speed. Then after two more weeks, I won the race! *Wow*! If Pepsi can't keep up with me, I must *really* be a fast runner, I thought! I'll just keep practicing my running every day, and I'll be the fastest runner in the world! I'll be an Olympic champion!

One day after we had raced, Pepsi flopped down on the cool kitchen linoleum floor beside her water dish, exhausted and panting, and mom noticed that Pepsi's belly and nipples were getting bigger. "Pepsi's pregnant!" mom announced. "You're not running *faster*, Pepsi's running *slower*," she said. *Darn*. So much for my running career.

The next time I got called into Mr. Fredericks' office, I still didn't have a career in mind, so I told him that I wanted to be a counselor, just like him. He smiled and was very pleased with that answer. Then again, who wouldn't be pleased by a kid that says he or she wants to follow in your footsteps? *He* was happy. *That* was the important thing, I thought.

Years later in high school I realized that I still didn't actually know what I wanted to be when I grew up, and time was running out. I was supposed to be thinking about college curriculums, but I was thinking about boys and clothes and hairstyles. I didn't know what I wanted to be. It was all just too confusing.

Choosing a career is such an important decision, and how is a kid to know what they do best? And career tests only indicate aptitude levels, not whether you'll actually enjoy doing the job day after day. Plus, you hear so many real-life stories about people who enter their chosen profession and hate it:

* Two psychology graduates, a man and his wife, earned master's degrees in psychology, set up a practice, and then decided that they hated being practicing psychologists. So they opened a small bakery. Turns out, they were much

happier baking bread and selling it to friends and neighbors than they were listening to other people's problems all day.

* A woman I met at a cocktail party two years ago told me that she earned a law degree and became a practicing defense attorney only to discover that she hated defending people that she knew were guilty. So she got a job working in a greenhouse and loves it. Because even though she spends a lot of time with her hands immersed in dirt, now she has a clean conscience.

* The minister at the church I used to attend in Houston was an eloquent speaker who could tell a heart-warming story so vividly there wouldn't be a dry eye in the room when he finished. The first time I met with him in his office to discuss joining the church, I asked him about his background. He was a certified plumber who at the age of 28 had made a small fortune but was still unhappy, he told me. So he went to divinity college and became a minister. It pays less money, but he's happier uplifting people's souls than he was unclogging people's pipes.

* My nephew recently graduated from college with a bachelor's degree in environmental science, and the only job he could find in the tight labor market was working part-time at the city zoo. Turns out, *that's* what he loves doing! He's always loved animals and is a volunteer at the local Humane Society. So now he's thinking about going back to college to earn a degree in biology or zoology.

It's easy to think about a profession and say, "I could do that," but you don't know whether you'll *like* doing something until you do it. That's why internships are so important. After working for years as an insurance clerk, a secretary, an executive secretary, a public relations assistant, a marketing coordinator and a radio news reporter, I finally decided at age 28 that I wanted to be a newspaper reporter. Enthusiastically I started attending college, and after getting an A in my first journalism class, I was offered a journalism internship working as a staff reporter for the college's student newspaper. I enjoyed the writing, won a journalism award and earned a journalism degree, but that internship made me realize that I didn't want to be a newspaper reporter. Then again, I know a woman who majored in public relations in college, started working as a public relations professional for a big corporation, hated it, and decided to try being a newspaper reporter. Turns out, that's what *she* enjoys.

A lot of people think it would be fun to own and operate a gift shop. I thought so until I volunteered for a charity in Houston and was asked to manage one of their gift shops. At first it was exciting, but once I learned everything, recruited a new stable of dependable volunteers and everything began running smoothly, it became boring. I worked there for two months, and when I announced that I was leaving, the manager of the Italian restaurant next door to the gift shop asked me how much the job paid because he had a friend who was looking for work. "Nothing!" I said. "I'm a volunteer." But at least I learned that I didn't like managing a gift shop *before* I took out a huge loan and actually opened one.

Now, years later, I know that being a freelance writer is what I do best and enjoy most, but I didn't realize that until I was 35 years old and actually quit my day job to do it full time. Turns out, I'm happiest working alone in an office in my home conducting research and telephone interviews and writing articles for news publications and magazines. Who knew?

But even if I *had* known at age 13 that I wanted to be a freelance writer, I'm quite certain the news would have stunned Mr. Fredericks. When he asked, "What career do you have in mind, Nancie?" if I had said, "I want to be a freelance writer!" he probably would have sighed deeply, gone home, cried to his wife "It's just *too* hard," and given up on career counseling. And I certainly wouldn't want *that* on my conscience.

The thing is, it's never too late to change jobs or professions if you're not happy. Many successful people, including real estate mogul Donald Trump, advocate that if you love what you're doing, you will be successful. In Trump's words, "you have to have a passion" for your work, or you should change jobs. The best example of that philosophy I know of is a photographer who got bored with taking pictures of weddings and portraits and created his own photography niche — taking black-and-white photos of women's naked breasts. The trend really caught on, because the women who hire him tell their friends about it. Now he has all kinds of women calling him because they want to hire him to photograph their breasts in an artistic way. Then they buy a snazzy picture frame and hang the photograph in their home, knowing most people won't recognize that it's actually *their* breasts. So it's their fun secret. Now *that's* creative — tweaking your current profession into a new niche — and there's a man who *really* looks forward to going to work every day!

*Nancie Hudson*

# Acknowledgments

In reflecting on this book, I would be remiss if I didn't thank the following people:

Dale, my husband, who suggested that I quit my job and become a freelance writer,

Dorothy Jean Hulst, my mom, who let me make huge messes in our house in the name of creativity and who taught me how to enjoy life,

Stu Boss, my dad, who taught me the art of storytelling and a strong work ethic, without which a freelance writer would never get anything done,

Steve Boss, my brother, who gave me my first subscription to *MAD Magazine*,

Ron Miazga, Professor of English, Kalamazoo Valley Community College, who taught me that no matter how good a first draft is, it can always be improved upon,

Michael Chevy Castranova, Editor of *Business Direct Weekly* and author of *A Perfectly Logical Explanation*, who inspired me to write a humor book,

And all of the people who told me their true, funny stories and trusted me to change all the names.

Thank you very much.

# About the Author

Nancie Hudson is an award-winning freelance writer. She has written hundreds of news and feature articles for national magazines such as *Health & Fitness*, *Cats*, *Environmental Protection* and *Hispanic Business Magazine*, regional business news publications such as *Business Direct Weekly* and *Enterprise*, and various trade journals and newspapers.

# Truth is *Funnier* Than Fiction II

Do you have a true, funny story that you would like to submit for Truth is *Funnier* Than Fiction II?

If so, please e-mail it to: nanciehud@aol.com (no attachments, please) or mail your typewritten story to:

> Nancie Hudson, Author
> c/o AuthorHouse
> 1663 Liberty Drive, Suite 200
> Bloomington, IN 47403

Printed in the United States
22189LVS00002B/337-438

9 781418 493660